LAST NIGHT ON
THE BEAT
BEST OF HARRY THE POLIS

. . .

HARRY MORRIS

BLACK & WHITE PUBLISHING

First published 2012
by Black & White Publishing Ltd
29 Ocean Drive, Edinburgh EH6 6JL

1 3 5 7 9 10 8 6 4 2   12 13 14 15

ISBN: 978 1 84502 456 7

A CIP catalogue record for this book is available from the British Library.

Typeset by RefineCatch Ltd, Bungay, Suffolk
Printed by Nørhaven, Denmark

...

Dedicated to my wee mammy Flora ... X

...

Also available from Harry the Polis

Even the Lies Are True
Even More Lies
Nuthin' Like the Truth
Ye're Never Gonnae Believe It!
Aye, That Will Be Right!50
Ah Cannae Tell a Lie
Up Tae My Neck in Paperwork
There's Been a Murder!
It Wisnae Me . . . Honest

Look Who's Up For A Blether
(DVD LIVE AUDIO PERFORMANCE)

This wee poem, to a lot of police officers in the service, epitomises what policing a community is all about. Therefore, I could not do a book with the Best of... and not include it. Everywhere I perform my stand-up shows, I'm asked to recite it.
Read on and see why!

I'm Just a Man Like You

. . .

I have been where you fear to be
I have seen what you fear to see
I have done what you fear to do
All these things, I have done for you
I am the man you lean upon
The man you cast your scorn upon
The man you bring your troubles to
All these men, I have been to you
The man you ask to stand apart
The man you feel should have no heart
The man you call the man in blue
But I'm just a man, just like you
And through the years, I've come to see
That I'm not what you ask of me
So take these handcuffs and this baton
Will you take it? Will anyone?
And when you watch a person die
And hear a battered baby cry
Then do you think, that you can be
All these things that you ask of me?
I'm just a man like you

Contents

. . .

Cheers Clarky

...

During my training at Tulliallan Police College, Jimmy Clark and I were always in trouble and regularly given punishment details. Not for anything bad, I might add.

One particular punishment was for parking in the wrong area. As Junior Division recruits, we were detailed to help out at the final qualifying-night 'party' being held for the senior division following their final passing-out parade.

This entailed Jimmy and I helping to serve them with their meal then, when they had finished eating, we would be required to clear the tables and collect all crockery and cutlery for washing.

During this part of the evening, all the senior division had entered the Crush Hall, where they had a bar and a disco set up.

Once we had finished clearing up, Jimmy and I were about to leave when we were instructed to attend at the Crush Hall and help the bar staff collect the empty glasses!

Under protest, we both attended and, as we entered, the party was winding down, although there was a good majority of them still on the floor dancing.

The tables were laden with drink as we both went about, weaving our way in and out with our trays, collecting the empty glasses.

At one table there were a lot of full glasses so Jimmy and I decided to clear up quicker by helping to empty them.

I had the whisky and Jimmy had the vodka.

Every time a table got up to dance, Jimmy and I would move in like the man in black in the Milk Tray advert and, during their absence, we would help relieve them of their hangover by draining their glasses for them!

It turned out to be one of the 'best' punishment details we were ever on… Hic! Cheers, Clarky! Hic!

Fatal Road Accident

· · ·

I once attended a fatal road accident, whereby, armed with a photo of the female victim, I attended her home address. I knocked on the door which was opened by her husband and showing him her photograph, I asked, 'Is this your wife?'

'Yes.' He replied immediately.

'Well, it looks like she's been hit by a bus!'

Too which he responded, Maybe so, but she's got a great personality!'

Polis Ansaphone

· · ·

I always wanted to record this and play it for a laugh.

'The Strathclyde Polis are not here right noo. So here is what we'd like you to do. Leave your name, your number and a message too and we will get right back to you….'

NAE CHANCE!

The Tasmanian Devil

...

During the World Pipe Band Championships at Bellahouston Park, in Glasgow, I was engaged in motorcycle patrol duties in the park when a young man, dressed in full Highland regalia, tartan kilt and all, approached my partner John Knox and myself and identified himself as a serving police officer from Tasmania, visiting Scotland to take part in the championships.

He asked if he could take a photograph of John and I on our police motorcycles, to which we readily agreed.

He then began to set up his camera, using a light meter and changing lens and filter.

While he did all this, I interrupted him and suggested he take his photograph from the opposite side, whereby he would also include all the competing pipe bands in the background with their variety of colourful tartans on display.

'Great idea'! He agreed.

He then proceeded to check the light meter again, changing the camera lens and filters for the new angle I had suggested.

Satisfied he had the correct lighting filters fitted, he began to focus his camera on us.

He then knelt down on the grass to capture his prized photograph, when – bonk! – in true commando-style Scottish-kilt-wearing, I witnessed a most unexpected surprise, as down from below his kilt and onto the grass below dropped his rather well-endowed penis!

This was definitely a 100-per-cent-genuine Tasmanian Devil!

If I didn't know better, I'd have sworn it was eating the grass!

As it was, it certainly appeared to be feeding on something!

At this point, two elderly women were passing and one of them an interest in what was happening with us.

On seeing the aforementioned exposed 'Tasmanian Devil' in full view and full colour, she grabbed hold of her friend's arm and in the loudest whisper I've ever heard, she said, 'Peggy! Peggy! Quick! Would you look at the size o' his cock? It looks like a wean's arm hanging oot a pram!'

Peggy turned around and looked on in amazement, then said to the young photographer, 'I bet you're not from around here, son?'

'No, ma'am,' he replied in a proud voice. 'I'm from Tasmania!'

'Of course you are and you're obviously eating your five a day 'cause you're a fine specimen of a boy!' Peggy said.

'Why thank you, ma'am!' he said, happily blushing.

'By the way!' Peggy added, 'you almost gave Cathy a stroke!'

'No he did not!' interrupted Cathy, then in a wicked girlie voice she said, But I wish he would have!'

Both women then walked off giggling like a pair of naughty young schoolgirls.

As for our Tasmanian police colleague, he was none the wiser as to what he had done, or the unexpected thrill he had bestowed upon two elderly Glasgow spinsters on a day out, strolling in the park!

However, I often wonder, thinking back to that day, if that is why all photographers, use the saying, 'Watch the Birdie!'

Don't Panic Missus Mannering!

· · ·

I attended a call from a young couple, reporting they had not seen their elderly neighbour, Missus Mannering, for some time.

She lived on the top-floor flat of a tenement building on the main street of Rutherglen.

I asked the usual questions of them, 'When was she last seen'?

'Three days ago, when she returned from a visit to her son who lives in Morecambe!'

'Has she any family relatives or friends up here?' I asked.

'No relatives, but she has a male friend who left to go back home, prior to us contacting you!' replied the neighbour.

How old is her friend and did he gain entry to the house?' I enquired.

'He's in his seventies and he was at the door for ages, trying to get in, but there was no reply!' he answered.

I then began knocking loudly on her door but, like her neighbours before me, there was no response from Missus Mannering.

The young couple was beginning to think the worse for their elderly neighbour.

I informed them, that the next step in the proceedings would be to consider using 'force' on her front door to gain entry.

The neighbours were in agreement with this course of action.

The door was large and solid with a decorative glass pane above it.

There were three locks fitted, but only one appeared to be in use.

I then performed the statutory polis action – by opening the letterbox and having a good sniff!

Now, I'm not sure why we always do this, because most old people have a certain smell about them, and without sounding disrespectful, I'm sure you know what I mean, but if you don't, it's that musty smell of Abernethy biscuits and piss!

Anyways, it looks good for the punters hanging around, before I get down to the real business of systematically demolishing the auld yin's nice door.

'Right, stand back please and give me some leg room,' I said, as I used all my force, coupled with my size 9 Doc Martens to boot the door lock.

I had to perform this action three or four times, before – crash! bang! wallop! – and the door burst open under my pressure.

As the door lock gave way, it swung open, then due to the force I had exerted, it crashed again, as the door safety chain that was fitted, broke, causing the door to strike a mirror hanging on the wall behind the door, dislodging it off the wall and culminating in it smashing into several pieces as it hit the floor.

Then, before the door swung back to the closed position, the decorative glass pane above it shattered due to the impact, raining glass down onto the stair landing.

Once the dust had settled, I entered the apartment, pushing the door and the broken wood and glass debris aside.

As I entered the hallway, I was stunned and surprised to see the small frail like figure of Missus Mannering, with a look of fear etched across her terror stricken face, standing halfway up the hall staring back at me.

I had to react quickly to calm the situation, so I put my hands up, in a typical Basil Fawlty-type manner, and like Clive Dunn's reassuring character, Dad's Army fashion when all appears lost, I shouted at her, 'Don't panic Missus Mannering! Don't panic! It's all right dear, it's just the police, checking to see that you're safe and well!'

'SAFE AND WELL!'

Her shocked facial expression gave the impression that I had rapidly accelerated her sell-by-date and she was about to drop down dead at my feet, there and then!

I then approached her, put my hands on her shoulders, spun her around and ever-so-gently, led her totally stunned and shocked tiny frail figure, towards the living room area. We were followed closely by the young couple, who appeared extremely awkward and embarrassed by what had occurred, due to their obvious concern for their elderly neighbour.

I made my apologies for the damage caused and quickly passed the buck by adding that I was acting on her young neighbour's advice and their genuine concern, that she may have suffered a sudden illness or fallen over, injuring herself.

I then asked the neighbour to make her a cup of tea and if possible, slip a couple of valium into it, as she appeared to be suffering from a severe shock to her system!

After some tea, accompanied by some welcome, comforting hugs and cuddles from the young female neighbour, (which I thoroughly enjoyed, to the annoyance of her husband). Only kidding, it was Missus Mannering she was cuddling.

With some TLC, Missus Mannering recovered from the terrifying surprise of her unexpected gatecrasher.

TLC in this scenario referring to 'The Loony Cop'!

I left in the knowledge that the young neighbour would replace the glass and effect the repair of the demolished door and locks.

This being the case, I wished them all the best.

They thanked me for my professionalism, after which I made a hasty Gung Ho retreat, whilst Missus Mannering was still breathing on her own, without any assistance.

However! Please don't let this story put you off contacting the police if you haven't seen your elderly neighbour for a few days.

Remember!—we are here to assist you, the public. It just might be a good idea not to call me!

Kids, You've Got To Love Them
. . .

A colleague of mine received appreciation letters from a local primary school, thanking him for showing them around the police station during their recent visit.

However, one letter stated, 'Thank you for letting me visit your police station. Until I met you and your police colleagues, I didn't know what a criminal really looked like up close'.

I do hope my colleagues did not confuse the child!

Fooled You

...

A good colleague of mine in the police had a twin brother working in another part of Glasgow.

Both brothers, Stewart and Clyde, were well known and instantly recognisable due to their appearance. They were, as we say in Glasgow, 'as black as two in the morning'!

On this particular night, Clyde was working in the Parkhead area of Glasgow and responded to a call, from an officer in the Bridgeton area requiring urgent assistance, with a serious disturbance, involving several youths fighting.

He made his way at speed in his police vehicle to the location and as he arrived, the youths responsible ran off in all directions.

The officers at the centre of the disturbance, signalled for Clyde to chase after the main instigator and trouble maker of the incident, pointing him out as he tried to make good his escape.

Clyde took to his heels and gave chase. Within a very short distance, he had caught up with the accused, who kept looking back, but could see nothing in the dark lit night.

After a few more strides, Clyde rugby tackled him around the waist and pulled him to the ground.

The accused was shocked and looked up at Clyde in total amazement with his eyes wide open and fear written all over his face!

He continued to stare at Clyde in utter shock and disbelief, while being handcuffed.

At which point Clyde stared him right in the face and said, 'What's up with you then? Never seen a Catholic before?'

Unisex Toilets

. . .

Occasionally, I get invited to the odd event: sports dinners, Burns suppers and charity fund-raisers so you can imagine my surprise when I was invited along to a celebrity VIP night, opening of a newly refurbished club/diner in the city centre.

Along I went on the night, smartly dressed in a suit and after the initial meeting and greeting certain faces I knew, I grabbed myself a couple of drinks and a plateful of hors d'oeuvres from the very impressive buffet selection made available to the guests.

After about an hour, I required to visit the little boys' room and was directed through by one of the many assistants on hand to help. But, little did I know this ultra-modern, fully refurbished establishment followed the latest trend across Europe – unisex toilets.

On entry there are mirrors and sinks on one side and smart looking cubicles on the other.

I promptly entered one before I met another user and had to make conversation. Once inside the cubicle I sat down on the impressive throne and was only settled down for a moment, when a female voice from the next cubicle said, 'Hi there!'

I looked either side of my cubicle before politely replying, 'Hi!'

'What are you up to?' She asked.

'Oh, just the same as you . . . I'm just sitting here.' I said.

'Is it okay if I come over?' She asked.

'Well eh, it's a bit embarrassing at the moment.' I responded.

Then her mood changed and she said, 'Listen Danielle, let me phone you back in five minutes, there's an idiot in the next cubicle answering all my questions!'

Cathy's Meals

• • •

As a serving police officer in Glasgow during the 1970s, many an accused person that I arrested in the south-side of Glasgow would genuinely plead with me to take them to Govan, or any other station for that matter, complaining about the food, loosely described as 'prisoner meals' and served up by the civilian female turnkey officer responsible for feeding them, whilst detained in police custody at Craigie Street.

Believing them to be exaggerating, I would never succumb to their request, but I was later to experience it for myself first hand and realise why I was continually asked.

It was during a stint, performing the duty of bar officer within Craigie Street Police Office, where I was responsible for checking the prisoners' welfare and safety while in my custody and making the female turnkey officer aware of how many of them were being detained for court the following morning and would therefore require to be supplied with a meal.

It was also considered a perk of the job as the bar officer, that if you wanted a cooked meal from her, you just let her know in advance and she would cook you a meal at the same time.

Most of the regular turnkeys at the various other police stations in our area, would make life simple for themselves by doing the easy thing and sending out to the local chip shop for fish and chips or sausage and chips in order to feed them, thereby using up the subsistence allowance they were allocated from the petty cash, to spend on each prisoner's meal.

However, the highly experienced and long term Cathy Carberry, who was a sister-in-law of the duty officer in charge and my specific female turnkey working with my shift, didn't agree to this and would insist in providing the prisoners in her care with some real home made family food!

Her description, not mine.

Also by doing this, she could save some money from the subsistence allowance she was allocated by the police in order to feed them, by cooking her meals in bulk. Definitely a cheaper alternative.

I walked into her kitchen and interrupted her during the preparation of one of her so called, real 'home made' family dinners and promptly announced:'That's another two prisoners just been detained in custody Cathy and the duty officer would like them to be fed, so that'll be nine customers you now have for dinner.'

Whilst making her aware of our updated guest list, I glanced down at the blue plastic plates spread out on her kitchen table to peruse her classic cuisine on offer.

Each plate contained of two slices of some sort of pink meat, which I could only crudely describe as resembling reject skin grafts from a hospital burns unit. It was so thinly cut I had to touch it to make sure it wasn't a photo copy she had thrown onto the plates to fool the unsuspecting prisoners.

With a limited amount of frozen potato chips spread around the plates there wasn't enough to disguise or hide the fact that the bottom of the plate was blue and to crown it all off, she had a pot of baked beans bubbling away on the gas ring.

'Well that's aw the frozen chips I have and I'm no' going out tae the shops at this time tae buy any mair and I'm buggered if I'm opening up another tin o' spam for them either. So sod it! It'll teach them for getting the jail at this time o' night!'

At that, she leaned over the table and began to lift chips from the plates she had previously set out and placed them onto the two extra plates. Spreading them out sparingly in an effort to make the plate look busy and cutting in half any big ones that were over a certain size.

She then lifted up the thinly sliced meat she had prepared earlier from each plate in turn and ripped a piece off each one, to add to the extra plates.

Finally, Cathy finished them off by counting the number of chips on each plate, making sure they were all equal with fourteen each, before plopping a spoonful of hot bubbling baked beans over them all, just to add a splash of colour and supplement the prisoners protein intake!

At this point, I might add, she put the loaves and fishes feast to shame by her distribution methods, carried out to perfection.

The final piece of Cathy's Culinary Cuisine came in the shape of a faded plastic blue mug and a slice of pan bread, a 'Basic' loaf from Tesco, at a cost of about twelve pence, with a scraping of cheap, tasteless margarine.

Now we are definitely not talking Jamie Oliver here. But 'Oliver'! maybe. . . and 'Gruel'! most definitely.

'I don't think I'm gonnae huv enough dinner tae feed you as well Harry!' she said apologetically.

'Don't worry about me Cathy, I'll just get by with a greasy fish supper out of Marini's chippie on the main street and think of what I might have had!' I replied condescendingly.

Although, I really wanted to say, 'Thank you Lord!'

"Will ye help me feed them"? She asked. As she poured what she described as their tea, into their individual blue plastic mugs.

Fortunately, or unfortunately, which ever way you look at it, several of the prisoners had been locked up in a cell all day and were so hungry, they would have welcomed a scabby cat 'atween two slices o' stale bread. But that wasn't on today's menu.

However, some of the other prisoners, who were more sceptical, scrutinised their plate and asked, 'Ho big man, whit is this ye're givin' me?'

'It's your dinner!' I replied, somewhat unconvincingly.

'My dinner? Are you having a laugh! I got the friggin' jail last night 'cause ah hit my wife for giving me a plate o' grub that was five times better than this shite!' Came back the reply, before continuing, 'Who's in the kitchen tonight, Fanny Craddock or that other fanny wi' his Atkin's diet?'

It was difficult to argue with him, however, the plastic mug of tea was the icing on the cake for many a prisoner that night.

'Whit is this pish ye're givin' us now big yin?' I was asked by a prisoner, staring into his blue plastic mug like a clairvoyant, desperate to see a tea leaf and find out if he had a future.

'It's your mug of tea!' I responded, somewhat hesitantly.

He looked at it intently for a moment and said, 'Frigging hell big man, when I was as weak as that, my wee mammy would sit up all night tae nurse me! There isnae any tea leaves in my mug tae confirm it is tea!'

Whoever came up wi' that load o' crap and called it a meal, must work for the Government, 'cause as long as ye're dishin' oot that load o' shite for prisoners grub, ye'll no' need tae bring back hanging as a deterrent, will ye?'

Fortunately, I believe the meals have improved since then but I believe Cathy came up with the concept for *Hell's Kitchen* before Gordon Ramsay!

Mind you! She might even be the forerunner that started the 5-a-day trend . . . Spam, Chips, Beans, Bread and Tea!

Tell It Like It Is!

• • •

I was standing at a check-out in Tesco, Silverburn, when a woman joined the queue behind me with a child of about 4 years-of-age.

The child was bawling her heart out and loudly screaming, 'Ah want my daddy . . . Ah want my daddy.'

The mother said, 'Ye cannae get yer daddy, noo shut up and eat yer sweeties!'

'Ah don't want sweeties, ah want my daddy.' The child repeated, through a mixture of tears and snotters.

'Well ye cannae get yer daddy.' The mother replied.

'How can ah no' get my daddy?' The distraught child asked.

To which the mother callously replied, 'Because yer daddy's fucked off back tae Poland . . . Noo eat yer sweeties and shut up!'

Nothing like breaking the news gently to the kids!

David Hay Said He Will Pay!

* * *

One of my favourite police motorcycle duties was escorting the various visiting football teams to Ibrox, Parkhead and Hampden Park in Glasgow.

On this particular occasion back in 1983, I was detailed to escort the English champions, Nottingham Forest, who arrived to play Glasgow Celtic in a European match.

I met with the Forest manager, undoubtedly one of the greatest of his era, Brian Clough, and introduced myself to him and vice versa.

Pleasantries completed, I then escorted the team through the city centre to Celtic Park for the game.

At the end of the game, I was outside the front door of the stadium waiting for the Forest team to appear and get back aboard their team coach, which would take them to Glasgow Airport, for their short flight home.

With all the players and officials safely aboard, I escorted them, blue lights flashing as we sped along the M8 motorway.

Suddenly, the coach driver began flashing his headlights and indicated he was pulling over onto the emergency hard shoulder.

I pulled over and stopped in front of the coach and was walking back to see what the problem was when the great man himself, Brian Clough, stepped off the team bus, approached me and asked if I knew where David Hay, the Celtic football manager, had his public house, in Paisley?

I replied that I did and Mister Clough asked if it was possible to make a detour past it, en-route to the airport, which I agreed to.

I carried on along the motorway, coming off at the exit that would take us along to David Hay's pub.

As we stopped opposite the front door, Brian Clough got off the team bus, crossed the road and went inside before returning to the bus moments later, he gave me the thumbs up to continue on our journey!

On our arrival at the Airport, Brian Clough came over and thanked me for my assistance, and I took the opportunity to ask him why he went in to David Hay's pub?

'Simple young man!' he replied in his illustrious voice. 'I ordered up drinks for everyone who was in the bar and told the staff to charge it to David Hay!'

Cheers for the memory Mister Clough.

Howard's Big Regret

. . .

I once had the pleasure of working with Howard Marks (Mr Nice) at the Blue Rooms in Liverpool.

Whilst sitting in our dressing room, waiting to go on stage, we were chatting away, to pass the time, when I asked Howard, 'What was your biggest regret, during all your drug trafficking?'

Howard sat for a moment, with glass of red wine in his hand, pondering over the question, when suddenly he raised his eyebrows, looked me straight in the face and said, 'Getting caught with your guys!'

On The Bus

...

I was sitting on the bus, when a young girl carrying a baby got on and sat down beside me.

Within minutes she had pulled out a breast and begun trying to breastfeed her baby.

I instantly looked the other way, slightly embarrassed by her action.

Then she said, 'Come on now, or I'll give it to this man sitting beside us!'

I immediately gulped, but couldn't resist having a second glance before looking elsewhere again.

Then moments later she said to her baby, 'Look, I'm warning you, if you don't take it this time, I'm going to give it to this nice man beside us.'

I couldn't hold back anymore, I had to intervene and said,

'Listen hen, do you think you could make up your mind, I was meant to get off the bus four stops back!'

Trampoline

...

Just bought a bed off Groupon from the makers of circus trampolines.

I might be wrong, but I think the wife will hit the roof!

Morris's Safety Motto

...

'Feel secure at night – sleep with a policeman!'

The Sixth Sense

· · ·

The other night, to pass the time, my partner was showing me some old videos of her friends and family, which had been taken at different functions over the past few years.

'That's my Aunt Isabel and my Uncle Robert. He died two years ago with a heart attack and she died not long afterwards! They reckon she had a broken heart.

'Oh, and see her with the blue hat on running up the path, that's my Aunt Ella. She's been widowed for years after my Uncle Sam died suddenly while they were on holiday in Turkey. They reckon it was food poisoning, but she couldn't prove it.'

'With names like Sam an' Ella? I'm not surprised!' I responded.

'There's my Aunt Ina with the red coat on. She was the one who died in her sleep and you went along with my mother to her funeral at Daldowie Cemetery! Do you not remember it?

'The stonemason spelt her name wrong on her headstone and put 'Ian' instead of Ina! They tried to blame her daughter for spelling wrong on the order form.

'And that's Agnes, who my mum goes to the bingo with and her man George. He suffered a massive heart attack. Poor old Agnes came in from the bingo and thought he was sleeping in the chair. What a shock she got when she tried to waken him up for his bed an hour later and found him sitting there, stiff as a board!

'Oh! and they two are Mary and Tommy who stayed across the road from my mum and dad. They both died of cancer, within a month of each other!' Shame! They both stopped smoking last year too!'

After five minutes of watching and listening to all this, I had to ask her to switch it off, I was getting so depressed. I felt like wee Haley Joel Osment in the Bruce Willis film, *The Sixth Sense*.

Everywhere I look . . . 'I SEE DEAD PEOPLE!'

Now That's Magic!
. . .

One evening, along with my partner Ewan Cameron, I was on mobile patrol, when I stopped a car for having a rear tail-light out.

I informed the driver why I had stopped him and he got out of his car and went to the rear to check for himself.

While doing this, Cameron walked to the front of the car to check for any other obvious defects.

The driver, meantime, on seeing the defective rear light, lifted his foot and kicked the light cover a few times, at which point, due to a 'short', caused by faulty wiring, the light came back on.

He then looked at me with a smug grin on his face and said, 'There ye go, as if by magic! It just needed a wee kick in the right place!'

At which point Cameron said, 'Good for you, mate. Now would you like to try that trick on your windscreen and see if you can get a valid tax disc to appear?'

Now, that really would be magic!

Wee Jock

• • •

I answered an advertisement in the local newspaper for a 'Small Scottish Terrier, free to good home, house-trained, but talks non-stop'!

I couldn't believe the last part of the advert so I called the telephone number given and spoke with the owner.

'No it's not a misprint!' He told me. 'You can come and see and hear it for yourself!'

This I just had to see! So I drove my car to the address given and the man whom I had spoken with a short time earlier on the telephone, answered the door to me.

'Ah take it you're here for the dog. Come away in!' He said.

As I entered the house he directed me toward a small terrier lying stretched out in a basket bed on the kitchen floor.

'Oh he looks great. What's his name?' I asked.

'His name?!' He repeated. 'Ask him. He can speak for himself.' At that the man turned around and left the room.

I felt quite silly at this moment. However, I turned to the wee dog which was now sitting up in his basket looking at me with his head cocked to one side and I said, 'So what's your name then?'

Without any hesitation, the wee dog answered back, 'It's Jock! Although, most people, him included, nodding his head towards his owner – refer to me as Wee Jock! A bit unfair mind you, considering I recently sired a big Doberman bitch two doors away!'

I stood there in total amazement. I couldn't believe it – a talking dog! I had to know more and hear his little Scottish voice answering all my questions.

'So tell me a bit about yourself, Jock! Like, how old are you? What's your background?'

'Awright! Pin yer ears back.' said Jock. 'When I was born, I was the wee runt in a litter of three. My mother never showed me any true love or attention and blamed me for my father running away with a border collie who just happened to work down the road at a nearby farm. She claimed it was my fault because he didn't want tae be associated wi' a wee runt like me.

'Anyways, she had a breakdown after this and went to the dogs, if you'll pardon the pun!

'She began hanging around with the homeless mongrel bitches in the area and getting involved in street fights as well as engaging in casual sex wi' the leader of the pack.

'My big brother Hamish spotted her having a gang bang with a boxer and his mates on a street corner. The dirty cow! Well wrong choice of species, but I'm sure you get my jist!

'As it was, I ended up being taken into care by a police dog handler, who brought me up with an alsatian called Rex and it wasn't long before I was allowed to go to work with him and very soon it became clear, I had a nose for sniffing out illegal substances!

'You name the drug, and I've snorted it! So to speak. I would go into an airport baggage hall and within minutes, I would have pin-pointed all the hold-alls, bags and suit-cases that contained even the least wee bit of gear. Aspirin! Hash! Coke! Within a very short period of time, I was the dog's bollocks. The chief constable awarded me commendation after commendation for the amount of illegal drugs I was finding and the number of crimes I was detecting.

'I was the Scottish Drug Squad's biggest asset!

'My handler used to joke that they should rename it the Scottish Dug Squad! After me.

'Here, check my basket by the way – it's full of police awards and rosettes. I was getting more publicity headlines than Lassie, in fact I was even collared and offered a film part in the re-make of Greyfriars Bobby, playing the lead, no less.

'Check my basket oot and read all the letters and fan mail I get. I'm not kidding you, and that's jist some o' it!

'Next thing I know, Her Majesty the Queen has contacted the chief constable, asking if I could come down to Buckingham Palace and sort out a few of her young royal corgis who were misbehaving, peeing and shitting all over one's Persian rugs and the carpets in the banquet hall. "Not a problem, Your Majesty", said the chief constable, seeing a knighthood in the offing. Within 24 hours, I was whisked off down to London to work in the palace.

'It was an absolute dawdle working for the royals and the food was pure nectar. The top chef was that Gordon Setter . . . or is it Ramsay? Y'know who I mean? Swears like a trooper.

'I sorted out the problem in jig time in my own sweet fashion by introducing a few of the cheeky corgi boys to my Glesca kiss and having a bite at another.

'I even took the opportunity to have a one-night stand and shagged one of them they called Fergie – she was a right randy wee bitch, but very accommodating. So, ye could say I've left a wee bit of Scottish bloodline among one's royal corgis.

'Mind you! I was CORGI registered! So I had authorisation.

'The entire episode was like nothing I'd ever experienced before, waking up every morning between Prince Phil and the Queen, I totally loved it and it didn't go unnoticed with Her (Majesty) indoors either, the job I had performed, teaching they young royal rascals a bit of etiquette à la Jock style.

'As a reward for all my efforts, I was recognised in her New Year Honours list. I'm sure you must have read about it! I was in all the newspapers, Wee Jock CBE, (Corgi Behavioural Expert), I was even pictured alongside big Sean Connery. He was a "shite for shore eyes!". That's one of the many impressions I do!

'However, if you don't believe me? Please! Check it out, it's all in my basket and it's officially stamped with the royal approval!'

I stood there full of intense anticipation and excitement, totally mesmerised by this fascinating wee dog. I was in awe of his incredible stories about his life.

'Please! Please Jock, carry on!' I pleaded. As I glanced over my left shoulder to catch a glimpse of his owner standing in the doorway, shaking his head in disbelief at my eagerness to digest more.

'Okay then!' Continued Jock. 'So I'm back home in Glesca, still working alongside the police Drug Squad, when all hell broke loose and I hear about the Iranian Embassy siege down in London.

'I couldn't believe what I was hearing on the news. This terrorist mob of murdering bastards were holding innocent people hostage! Sorry for swearing boss, but I was barking mad, if ye get my drift!

'Anyhow, the door burst open and in walked the chief constable, Sir David. "Jock!" he shouted. "Prime Minister

Thatcher has been on the telephone and she wants you down at the Iranian Embassy asap, to work in conjunction with the elite SAS in a covert operation."

'Will they gie me a gun? Will they gie me a gun? I pleaded with him. Oh please, gie me a gun and let me shoot the buggers!

"Can't do it Jock!" he said. "We're British, it's not our way. Anyways, the SAS have a special assignment in mind that only you can do! Even I don't know what it is. So, good luck Jock. Go forth and do us proud, son!" He then lifted me up onto his knee, gave me a cuddle, rubbed noses with me, patted me on the head and said "I love you Jock, take care wee man!"

I got a bit worried about that last remark, 'cause I've never seen him look at me like that before, never mind uttering the words "I love you". 'Anyway, I was whisked away to Glesca Airport to be flown down south first class, where I was met by Maggie's private secretary and a driver. All very top secret, but that's the way it had to be . . . '

'Aw hurry up, for God's sake!' interrupted Jock's owner.

'Hey, you!' said Jock. 'Keep it shut or I'll tell him about the special DVDs' you hide under yer bed for night-time viewing!'

The owner clamped up and stepped back out of the doorway.

'Right now, where was I before I was so rudely interrupted?' asked Jock.

'You had arrived in London and were being driven to the hostage siege at the embassy.' I replied excitedly, fully engrossed in every bit of his story.

'Oh, aye! Well, I arrived there and was taken to see the PM and her commander in chief, who was directing the operation. "Jock!" he said, recognising me instantly from my photos in the paper and delighted to see me. Then putting his arm around me, he ushered me over.

"Here's what we want you to do."

'He then explained they were going to fit a small video camera to my collar after which I would wander over and locate the cat flap at the rear door of the embassy. Once there, I would enter the embassy building and casually walk around the various rooms and floors, videoing the terrorists and their positions within the offices for the information of the SAS. As an added extra, whilst carrying out this task and being virtually unnoticed by the terrorist bastards, I was to casually piddle down the left leg of every one I came across, marking them with my urine!

'Now the boys in the SAS, for their part, would burst in wearing special night-sight, pish-detecting goggles that would show up my urine like a luminous yellow stain, thereby identifying the bastards to be shot. Easy-Peasy!

'So off I went, through the door and as I walked up to the first big mother f****r, nice as you like, I lifted my leg and skooshed him. Not one of them paid any notice to me, as I wandered about the rooms amongst them like a ghost though one o' the manky bastards did try to entice me o'er with a chocolate biscuit. But he was pure mocket and had black teeth so I just kidded him on I was friendly, then had a quick skoosh o'er his leg, before buggering off sharpish.

'After the initial few squirts down the leg of the ones I'd met, I was getting right into my stride. Showing some neat versatility in the process.

'I was ambidextrous and displayed a variety of special moves, lifting either leg to skoosh the bastards. Left leg, right leg. I got carried away that much, I fell over a couple o' times, trying tae lift both my legs at the same time.

'I kept this up, sometimes double-dunking a particular big diddy that I really disliked, just to make sure he was a target and not mistaken for one of the good guys.

'I continued in this vein until, inevitably, I had completely emptied my tank! I was dehydrated. Now running on empty, I made my way back out, armed with my video pictures of some right pishy-looking terrorists and gave it to the boys of the SAS to view, before preparing to storm the embassy. As soon as they entered, they couldn't miss the terrorists and their bright yellow left legs. I couldn't have done better. It was as if I'd stuck a poster on each one stating, "Shoot me, I'm a baddie."

'As a result, it was all over in minutes, with the terrorists overpowered and not a hair on a hostage harmed. Thanks to me!

'The Prime Minister was ecstatic! She couldn't believe that Operation Iranian Embassy had gone so smoothly. She cuddled me! Denis breathed whisky on me and that Kate Adie couldn't keep her hands off me – desperate for me to give her one! An exclusive story that is! But I kept shtoom!

'I ended up back at the palace getting awarded with a bravery medal from the Queen who, along with Prince Philip was delighted for me.'

Totally amazed with his wonderful stories, I turned to Wee Jock's owner standing in the hallway and said, 'Why would anyone want to get rid of this wee heroic dog, his stories about his life are totally amazing?'

At which point, his owner put his hands up to his head in sheer frustration and anguish before screaming:

'It's the LIES! I just can't stand his BLOODY LIES!'

My Deaf Wife . . .
. . .

Recently, I've felt that my missus wasn't hearing as well as she used to, and thought she might be needing a hearing aid. Not quite sure how to approach her, I contacted our family doctor to discuss her problem.

The doctor told me there was a simple informal test that I could perform in order to give him a better idea about her hearing loss.

'Here's what you do,' said the doctor. 'You stand about twenty feet away, and in a normal conversational speaking voice, ask her a question and see if she hears you.

'If she doesn't respond, go to fifteen feet, then ten feet, and so on until you get a response.'

That evening, my missus was in the kitchen preparing the dinner, and I was in my wee office. So I thought to myself, 'I'm about twenty feet away, I'll try out what the doctor suggested and see what happens.'

Then in a normal speaking tone I asked her, 'Darling, what's for the dinner?' . . . No response.

So I decided to move up closer to the kitchen, till about fifteen feet away from her and repeated, 'Darling, what's for the dinner?' Still no response.

Next, I moved into the dining room where I was only about ten feet from her and I asked her again, 'Darling, what's for the dinner?' Again I got no response.

So, I walked up to the kitchen door, about five feet away and said. 'Darling, what's for the dinner?'

Just like my previous attempts there was no response.

Finally, I walked right up and stood behind her and said. 'Darling what's for the dinner?'

To which she turned around to face me and replied rather irately, 'For the fifth time Harry, . . . It's f*cken MINCE!'

It's In The Stars

• • •

My old mate Jimmy Clark and I were on patrol duty one evening, parked within a pedestrian precinct, in Glasgow, when I recognised a well-known female clairvoyant/fortune-teller, coming out of a restaurant, where a charity celebrity dinner was being held by astrologers, clairvoyants and psychos . . . Sorry, psychics!

We watched her as she unsteadily made her way over to a parked vehicle, opened the door and got into the driver's seat.

She started the vehicle up and promptly reversed it into a concrete plant pot in the precinct, before driving off.

We quickly followed her out and after a short distance, signalled for her to pull over and stop. As I suspected, she was driving under the influence of alcohol.

I informed her of my suspicion and proceeded to give her a breath test, which proved positive.

As procedure dictates, I informed her, 'I arrest you!'

She then looked Jimmy straight in the eye with a bewildered, glazed expression on her face and said in all sincerity, 'What is going to happen now?'

To which Jimmy couldn't resist replying, 'You're the clairvoyant-you tell me!!'

Guess My Age!
• • •

This is one of those stories you hear over the years that you just have to include for old time's sake, if nothing else.

Old Tommy Boyd, an elderly retired cop, was fed up looking in the mirror every morning at his heavily lined, baggy eyes and drooping excess skin on his ageing face. So one day, whilst reading an article on cosmetic surgery, he decided to withdraw some of his hard earned savings from his bank account and do something about it.

He rang the number in the advert and requested an initial appointment, to see a specialist consultant regarding some facial surgery.

After the consultation with the cosmetic surgeon and his assurances of what he could do for him, coupled with the promise that he would look much younger afterwards, Tommy decided, 'What the Hell'! And booked up with the surgeon to go ahead and have it done.

Several weeks later, after the superficial scarring disappeared from his facial surgery, old Tommy – sorry, 'young' Tommy – decided it was time to literally face the outside world with his new look.

Dressed to kill and looking very dapper in his best suit, collar and tie, Tommy made his way down the main street, stopping off at the local newsagent's shop.

'I'll have a Daily Record please, Martha'. he said to the female counter assistant.

The counter assistant looked at him as she handed over the paper and said, 'I'm terribly sorry sir, but do I know you'?

'Of course you do Martha, it's me – Tommy Boyd!' he replied.

'Good God, Tommy Boyd!' she remarked. 'I didn't recognise you. You look absolutely fantastic in fact, you look about forty years-of- age!'

A very proud Tommy responded, 'Well I'm actually sixty-seven years old!'

'That's incredible, Tommy, you're looking truly amazing!' she said.

After some further small talk, Tommy left the newsagent to continue his shopping.

As he walked along past the shops, he stopped off and entered the butcher's shop.

While standing in a queue, he couldn't resist tapping the shoulder of the woman in front of him and asking her, 'Excuse me hen, but what age do you think I am?'

The woman looked Tommy up and down before commenting, 'Ye're about forty-five, forty-six'! She replied confidently.

This prompted Tommy to ask the butcher behind the counter, to have a guess.

'I'd say you're probably between forty-two and forty-five years of age.' said the butcher.

Smiling proudly and totally delighted with the responses, Tommy replied, 'Well ye're both wrong. I'm actually sixty-seven years old!'

The people in the butcher shop were amazed at his youthful looks and there were several 'oohs' and 'aahs' amongst them.

A short time later, after being served, Tommy left the butcher shop and jauntily walked down the road to the nearby bus stop to await the arrival of a bus, to take him into the city centre for the first time in months.

Standing there waiting and completely ecstatic with the response his new look appearance was attracting, Tommy decided to ask the only other person in the bus shelter, an elderly woman, dressed in a tweed coat, rain-mate and with her shopping trolley. 'Excuse me missus, but do you mind if I ask you a personal question'?

'Not at all son.' She replied, agreeing to his request. 'Ask away.'

'How old do you think I am?' he asked.

The elderly woman looked intently at him, pausing for a brief moment, before answering, 'I'm not really sure son. I'd need to feel yer boaby to be able to tell ye exactly!' she replied.

'Feel my boaby? D'you mean my penis?' responded a surprised Tommy.

'Aye yer boaby! Penis! Tadger! Nob! Cock-a-doodle-doo! Whitever ye want tae call it.' Said the old woman. 'That is if ye have one and ye really want me to guess yer age exactly right!'

Confident he could comply with this unusual request, Tommy agreed, 'Right hen, you're on!'

Tommy slipped his trouser zip down and the elderly woman inserted her hand through the opening in his underpants and grabbing hold of his penis, she then fondled and rolled it around in her hand, having a right old grope at it, before taking her hand back out of his trouser opening.

Tommy promptly zipped up his trousers and said, 'Right, my age!'

'I'm no' very sure!' she said. 'I'd need to feel yer testes!'

'My testes'? Tommy enquired. 'What's my testes?'

Quick as a flash the elderly woman said, 'Aye, yer testes!

Ye know, yer bollocks! The place where awe you men keep a nursery full of potential screaming weans! Mind you that is if you want me tae guess yer age exactly right!'

Tommy thought for a moment, then relented, 'Okay, then, have a feel at my testes if you think it will help you guess my age exactly right!'

The elderly woman performed the same procedure, this time grabbing his bollocks and rolling them around in the palm of her hand like the Humphrey Bogart character with stress balls in *The Caine Mutiny*.

After several minutes, she withdrew her hand.

At this, Tommy zipped up his trousers, after which, he composed himself before asking, 'Well. What's your guess then? How old am I?'

After a moment's pause the elderly woman blurted out with complete confidence.

'Ye're exactly sixty-seven years old, ya silly auld bugger!'

Tommy is totally stunned and shocked by this reply.

'How the hell did you know that?' he asked her.

'Dead easy!' replied the elderly woman. 'I was in the queue at the butcher's!'

What's He Like?

• • •

Whilst walking through a busy shopping mall one day, a young boy came running over to me with tears in his eyes and said, 'I've lost my daddy!'

'What's yer daddy like son?' I asked him.

The young boy thought for a moment then said, 'Horse racing and drinking whisky!'

A reply that describes an awful lot of daddies in Glesca!

Little Arrows

* * *

I once had the privilege of meeting and providing a motor-cycle escort for Sir Elton John, to his concert performance at the SECC, Glasgow.

I was instructed to go to the Holiday Inn hotel and meet him and his manager, John Reid, to arrange a time for him to be picked up for his show.

I met with John Reid first in the lobby of the hotel and was taken upstairs by him to be introduced to Elton, whom I found to be an extremely polite, friendly and hospitable person.

While I was there Elton showed me his large, mobile wardrobe, filled to the brim with his spectacularly flamboyant, colourful and over-the-top stage costumes, which I must admit were very impressive.

'Tell you what, I'll pick out something special to wear tonight Harry, for when you come to pick me up!' he said, as I was leaving his hotel room.

I have to admit I was somewhat surprised at his jocular and friendly attitude towards me and was even more surprised later that evening, when I turned up to escort Elton and he came walking out of the front door of the hotel dressed in a convict-style uniform and hat, brown in colour and decorated with the little black arrows all over it!

I stood there somewhat taken aback as he approached me, and as he got closer, he threw his arms out by his side and said:

'HOWZAT HARRY!'

It's In The Bag

. . .

I received a call one day to attend a large superstore in Renfrew Road, Paisley, regarding a male detained for shoplifting.

On my arrival at the store, I spoke with the store detectives, who witnessed the theft and obtained the necessary statements.

I then asked the store security, 'What did the accused steal?'

'A lawnmower grass box.' Replied the witness.

I then met with the accused shoplifter and had to satisfy my curiousity, so I asked him, 'Why are you stealing a grass box?'

The shoplifter boldly replied, 'Off the record boss, I'm a professional shoplifter and between you and me, I blagged the lawnmower yesterday for a punter, but I didnae notice there was a grass box wi' it, so I came back today tae get it and I reckon some bastard grassed me to the store security in the car park!'

'How much do you earn shoplifting?' I asked with interest.

'I make a good living, stealing to order!' he replied proudly.

Puzzled by his cocky response about the grass box, I had to ask him how he had managed to walk out of a store with a large power lawnmower without anyone in security noticing?

He winked at me and replied, 'If I tell you that boss, you'll want my job!'

I then winked back at him, placed my handcuffs on his wrists and said, 'Don't think so mate!'

Mini's a Bargain!

. . .

Being recognised as a bit of a scatter-cash when it comes to spending money, it came as no surprise that there was no expense spared when it came to purchasing my first real motor car.

There it was, in the paper, circled with a fancy 3D box, with the bold heading to make it stand out from the rest stating, 'Bargain Of The Month!'

I liked the name right away, a Morris Mini, brown in colour and all for the princely sum of £30 cash, from the Executive Car Centre, Paisley!

On opening the driver's door, the pungent smell of dampness should have been an obvious clue, but I accepted the salesman's enthusiastic patter, 'Can ye no' smell that leather upholstery? Man, ye just cannae beat the real McCoy. None o' yer cheap shite here.' He enthused before adding. 'And another wee extra feature fitted, is the sporty bucket-style racing seats!'

They were certainly bucket seats all right! Saturated with water and the metal rimmed handle still attached!

There was a 'Hole in dem bucket seats, dear Henry, dear Henry'!

The radio wasn't working either, but he put it down to a faulty valve, or maybe a short wire!

In other words, I think it was a wire – less! Definitely something missing that's for sure.

'Don't worry sir, we'll replace it!' he said with an air of confidence. 'Are we paying by cash here, or would you like me to fix up credit arrangements?' he enquired.

'None of your HP credit payments for me', I said, handing over my hard cash! £6 of which was made up with crisp new 10-shilling notes from my unopened police pay packet.

With the ignition key thrust into my hand, I jumped into the driver seat and started it up!

In an instant, I noticed there was no 'va va voom!' It was more like a 'buzz buzz buzz!' For a brief moment I thought there was a wasp stuck up the exhaust pipe, but no, that was the noise from my souped-up, (clapped out) mini engine.

'Just listen to that engine man, it's purring like a cat!' said the drooling salesman with his syrup of fig hairpiece, slightly askew.

'Purring like a cat' my arse! It was more like 'squealing like a pork belly pig!'

The noise emanating from under the bonnet, suggested a slack fan belt. Or in my case, probably a slack snake belt!

Even the MOT certificate turned out to be a duplicate. The examiner obviously didn't believe it the first time!

However, I put all that to one side as I drove out onto the main road.

Let's see what this baby can do, I thought. nought to sixty in eight the salesman said, he forgot to mention days and not seconds.

I should have remembered a favourite old saying of my father's: 'The only good thing about Paisley, son, is the main road leading out of it to Glasgow!'

Well, I was on it and I was eager to burn some rubber.

Forget Michael Schumacher – he was just a 'Cobbler' from the Govan area when I was at school.

With the pedal to the metal, I was off in a large puff of smoke. So much so, I actually expected a genie to appear from behind the dashboard and grant me three wishes.

Like, 'I wish I had an engine', 'I wish I was a mechanic' and thirdly, 'I wish someone would kick me in the testicles and give me a wake up call.' helloooo!

Well it was the pantomime season after all. (Oh yes it was!)

Having been on the road now for just over thirty minutes, enough time to go home and back on a bus and driving flat out, I finally came across a sign for Glasgow.

The art of prayer really does work.

Now, I know a Mini engine is not the most powerful, but this one of mine, wouldn't pull a sailor off yer granny! Suffice to say, I would have been hard pushed to pull the skin off my Ambrosia creamed rice pudding!

A man and woman on a tandem bike and an old woman, pulling herself along in a wheelchair, with one leg and a punctured tyre overtook me twice!

Come to think of it, maybe the holes in the floor of my car were for my Doc Marten boots to go through, so I could run and make it go faster! Then again, maybe they were part of the braking system.

Suddenly, it began to rain quite heavily and I switched on the windscreen wipers . . . Nothing! Zilch! Nada! Zero!

In layman's language, they didn't work and as the rain got heavier, it became more difficult to see the road ahead.

Drastic times require drastic measures, as I rolled down my window, put my hand out and grabbing hold of the wipers, I began operating them manually, thrashing them up and down the windscreen. Not recommended!

To cut a very long story short, I decided not to hold onto it for too long. Depreciation in value and all that.

So, while I was still a student at the Police College, Tulliallan, I was offered the chance to purchase another

Mini, this time from sergeant Colin Robertson, who was a college instructor.

As we say in Glasgow, it was 'minted' and into the bargain, the purchase might secure me some much-needed brownie points with the seller! So, after checking that the window wipers worked properly, I bought it!

Here I was, twenty-one years of age and the Jeremy Clarkson of Govan, coupled with the fact, we were the first two-car family in the street. Mind you, there were only two houses: it was an awfy wee street I lived in.

Was I becoming an obsessed collector of cars, I thought?

As it was, Dougie Mack, a fellow student, just happened to be looking for some form of transport himself and practically begged me to sell my manually operated spare Mini.

Without too much persuasion, I managed to convince him, to talk me into selling him, my wee brown passion wagon.

'OK! OK!' I said, reluctantly. 'Give me thirty quid cash and she's all yours!'

'Why call it 'she' you might ask? 'Cause it was an absolute cow in the morning! And the rest of the bloody day I might add. I had to tinker about with the engine just to start it. It was like performing foreplay every time I went into it, before I could get 'her' to do anything!

However, Dougie was a single guy and had money burning a hole in his pocket, so I couldn't help but smile, when driving down the motorway on my way home from the Tulliallan Police College, for the weekend, when I was overtaken by Dougie, waving away frantically and blasting the horn with great excitement, as he passed.

I think that was the first time it had passed anything.

I tell a lie, it once passed water on the day the radiator hose burst, but therein lies another story!

On returning to the police college the following Monday, I had to laugh, when I asked Dougie how the car was running and he informed me, it had been scrapped!

'Scrapped?' I said, somewhat hesitant and surprised.

'Aye. Ah gave a burd a lift home from the dancing on Friday night and as I was reversing back, listening to 'Suzi Quatro' on the radio, when I collided with an 'Audi Quattro in the car park!'

'Whit! Her husband?' I enquired.

'Naw ya numpty! Another motor in the car park. A bashed in the driver's door. That cost me an arm and a leg', he added.

'What about your damage?' I asked, trying to sound concerned.

'My damage?' he replied. 'The bloody sub-frame collapsed and dropped down, but the burd was a darling, so, I ignored it and drove along a country road and parked up, in a field for a wee winching session, while we listened to Wet Wet Wet. As it was, it turned out to be more like 'Pish Pish Pish!' as the rain became heavier and poured down.'

'Later, as I went to drive away, the ground was that soft with all the rain, the bloody motor had sunk and was now up to its axles in mud.

So, there we were, stuck fast in the mud and so I had walk it to the nearest house to call out Newbridge Vehicle Recovery, who attended and proceeded to 'rip' me off along with the rest of the sub-frame, as he towed my Mini out of the field.

'Total cost for my weekend: thirty quid to you for the motor, a hundred quid to the Audi Quattro driver for the damage to his door and forty quid for the recovery driver and as if that wasn't bad enough, I never even got my Nat King Cole!'

As he stood there staring at me, I said sympathetically, 'Ah well Dougie, some people are just lucky with cars! Some people are just lucky in love! But unfortunately for you Dougie my son . . .'

I paused for a moment, before saying, 'You've just got too much money!'

Name That Tune

· · ·

My colleague Ian Whitelaw from the Strathclyde Police Pipe band was telling me in conversation that they are to release a new CD of Scotland's finest bagpipe tunes. The only hold up is, what to call it.

Without the least bit hesitation I suggested, 'How about Criminal?'

Will Power!

· · ·

I'd just come out of the chippy with a meat and potato pie, large chips, mushy peas a jumbo sausage and two pickled onions, when a wee homeless man sitting outside, looked up at me and said, 'Here mate. I've not eaten for two days!'

I looked down at him with admiration and said, 'I just wish to f**k I had your bloody will power pal!'

Donald & Johnny Ramensky

. . .

There was I performing my nightshift duty, reading over my police reports when the main door of the front office was opened and in walked an elderly male. Slightly gaunt in appearance and stooping forward, I instantly recognised him as Donald Lindsay, a former police colleague of mine and now, long retired from the old City of Glasgow force of several years ago.

'Hello Donald!' I said, putting my hand out to shake his. 'How are you mate?' I asked, delighted to see him after so long.

Donald looked at me with a blank, vacant look on his face and said,

'Do you know me mister?'

'Of course I know you; you're Donald Lindsay and I'm Harry Morris. We worked together. Surely you remember me?'

My response went right over Donald's head and he said, 'I can't find my gloves and I need to wear them when it's cold or my hands get sore. Have you got my gloves?'

I quickly realised that Donald was ill and within a very short time, I learned that he was missing from a south-side Nursing Home, where he was being treated for dementia.

As I sat alongside Donald, keeping him occupied, while awaiting the arrival of staff from the nursing home, my thoughts took me back to our days at Craigie Street Police Office. Donald had spent most of his police service there and I always looked upon him as a very smart, polite and knowledgeable officer, of whom I searched out on numerous occasions to ask his advice on a particular police matter.

On one of the occasions I was fortunate to be partnered off with Donald, working alongside him on the Divisional Crime car, he related this story to me about one of the best known criminal 'safe crackers' in Britain, called Johnny Ramensky, the son of a Lithuanian immigrant to Scotland, whom he had the task, along with his partner Bert Gordon, of escorting from the Glasgow High Court to Peterhead Prison, after his brief appearance at court for the last time, to appeal against his latest custodial sentence.

Often referred to as 'Gentleman Johnny', because he never displayed any violence towards anyone when arrested, his crimes were always that of breaking into premises and opening and removing the contents of their 'safe'!

An art of 'safe-breaking' that Johnny performed rather well, in fact, unfortunately for him, it was rather too well, in respect that his expertise work was instantly recognisable by the police and he was subsequently arrested within a few days of the crime being discovered.

It was also an open secret that in 1942 when war was raging across Europe and whilst languishing in a prison cell, as a guest of HMP Peterhead that Johnny wrote a letter to the government requesting that his undoubted skills be utilised and put to good use.

Johnny was ecstatic when his request was accepted and he was seconded into a special commando unit led by General Lacey and dropped behind enemy lines, in order to use his mercurial ability to break into German Officers safes and remove all secret documents required to assist the war effort.

He was asked to perform a similar operation during the fighting in Italy, where, as one of the first troops into

Rome, he blew open and removed all the contents of fourteen foreign embassy safes in one day, including one belonging to Hermann Goering, the Nazi military leader.

During his brief appearance in Glasgow for his latest court appeal, he was allowed a private visit from his family, who were present, before being placed in the rear of the police car and driven off on the long journey back up to Peterhead Prison.

It was during the long and tedious journey in heavy traffic that they decided to stop off for a break and change of driver.

Johnny had intimated he was 'choking' for a drink and he also required to visit the toilet.

Donald pulled off the road into the car park of a Country Tavern and as they were about to apply the handcuffs on Johnny in order to convey him inside to the toilets, Johnny sighed and said.

'Here guys, why do you have to do this to me when I need to pee? Why you not let me go in myself without you and your uniforms and I will buy the drinks for us to enjoy?'

Donald and Bert looked at each other and deliberated for a moment. They both knew, under the circumstances they could not enter the licensed premises in uniform and enjoy the thirst quenching delights of a cool beer on this warm day.

However, in the short time they had spent together in Johnny's company, they had formed a mutual relationship and Johnny always displayed the utmost respect and admiration for the police and the difficult job they performed on a daily basis.

'Please guys, trust me!' Johnny pleaded.

However, having listened to Johnny's reassurances, Donald and Bert looked at each other and agreed to his offer. After all, it would be the last time Johnny would get the opportunity to visit a pub of any description, for quite some time.

'Okay!' Donald said, putting his hand into his pocket. 'Here's some money to buy the beers, but don't let us down Johnny!'

Johnny assured him he had nothing to worry about and taking possession of the money, he casually walked towards the door of the Tavern and disappeared inside.

Bert quickly rushed over to a window at the side of the Tavern to try and observe what was taking place with Johnny, before returning to the police car.

As they both waited patiently outside, Johnny appeared in full view, larger than life, walking toward them like a free man, albeit for a brief moment, from the door of the Tavern, carrying three tins of Pale Ale.

He walked straight over to the unmarked police car handed them over to Donald.

Donald took possession of the beers, but a look of disappointment came over his face, as he looked at Bert and said.

'Tin opener! No tin opener. How are we going to open them?'

'Not a problem'. Said Johnny, interrupting him, he placed his hand inside his jacket pocket and handed over a small metal tin opener. 'It was lying on the bar just asking to be lifted!'

'Johnny!' Donald said. 'You'll get us all the jail for stealing!'

Taking it from him, Bert opened each tin and handed them out.

As Donald took a swig from his can he couldn't hide his obvious pleasure.

'Ahhh! That's brilliant, but in all honesty, I would have preferred to drink it from a cool pint glass, rather than out a tin!'

No sooner had Donald uttered these words, when Johnny produced two pint tumblers from the inside pocket of his jacket.

As Donald and Bert looked at him for an explanation, Johnny replied dismissively, 'They were also lying on the bar just asking to be lifted!'

A short time later, their thirst fully quenched, they continued with their duty of escorting 'gentleman' Johnny Ramensky to his final home, HMP Peterhead.

Donald just loved telling that story about him, Bert and Johnny.

Several months after our meeting that night, sadly, my former police colleague Donald Lindsay passed away peacefully in his nursing home in Glasgow.

All Bets Are Off

• • •

'Tank' was a 'scrap metal man' and likeable rogue from the Bridgeton area of Glasgow, who received some unexpected bad news when visiting the Cardiology Department of the Royal Infirmary for a check-up.

It appeared he was required to undergo immediate triple heart bypass surgery and the doctor wanted him admitted no later than the following day.

Tank informed some of his close friends regarding his news and the following scenario, is the reaction he received from his old Bridgeton buddies.

'Gonnae gi'es yer motor? Seeing that ye'll probably die during the operation!' Remarked Wee Dougie.

'Naw, ah will not!' Replied a confident Tank.

'Ye might. It's a serious operation that bypass.' Came back Dougie.

'Nae chance!' Said Tank, lighting up a cigarette. 'I'm as strong as a hoarse!'

'Right then!' Said Dougie. 'I'll bet you, ye die in the operating theatre!'

'I'll bet ye I frigging don't!' Replied a confident Tank.

'Ye're on. Ah say ye will and you say ye won't. How much?' Enquired Dougie.

'I'll bet ye a Tenner!' Said Tank. (That's £10.00 in money)

'Ye're on!' Replied Dougie.

At that, they both licked their thumbs and rubbed them together sealing the £10 bet.

A couple of days later, Tank underwent his triple bypass operation.

Afterwards, he was wheeled out into the recovery room before being admitted into the intensive care unit for observation.

Wee Dougie, on hearing Tank had gone through his operation, contacted Tank's wife and enquired how he was and asked if he could visit him in Hospital.

Tank's wife informed Dougie that the operation had gone well and that he was in the ICU, but visiting was restricted to close family members only.

Wee Dougie was concerned about his good friend and decided to con his way into the hospital ward, to pay Tank a visit and see for himself.

As he arrived at the ICU, he informed the nursing staff that he was there to visit his older brother and was directed down to the far end of the ward, where Tank was.

Dougie, slightly apprehensive as to how is old friend would be, began his slow walk down the ward towards Tank.

As he got closer to the bed, he could see several metal stands and bright monitors all around him, with various tubes leading from them, going into Tank's body where he is lying with his head to one side and his eyes closed, apparently asleep.

On seeing all this highly technical monitoring equipment, Dougie nervously bent over the hospital bed to look at Tank's face and, as he did, Tank opened one eye, looked straight at Dougie's face, put his hand out in front of him and with total conviction said, '**TENNER!**'

Who Was That?

. . .

Whilst working within the police motor vehicle garage at the start of my traffic patrol officer career, I was being shown all the various parts of a car engine, what can go wrong and how to repair it. Like I was remotely interested!

However, later the same day, I was finished my shift and walking down to the end of the garage, when the wall telephone started ringing.

The garage sergeant shouted, 'Do me a favour Harry and answer that!' So I went over and picked it up and the following is what took place.

'Helen Street police garage, can I help you?'

'Yes you can,' replied the caller. 'You can tell me what is happening with the nightshift superintendent's car?'

'I'm sorry mate, but I have absolutely no idea what's happening with it!' I replied.

To which the caller responded, 'Do you know who you are speaking with?'

No!' I replied, before adding. 'So who am I speaking to?'

'You are speaking with Superintendent White!' He said in a voice of authority.

I paused for a moment, and then asked him, 'And do you know who you're speaking to!'

'No I don't', he answered.

To which I replied, 'Good!' And promptly put the telephone down.

As I walked away, the garage sergeant enquired, 'Who was that Harry?'

'Wrong number sarge!' I replied, before quickly walking off.

The Heilan' Coo!
• • •

A few years ago, back in the days of the City of Glasgow Police Force. A newly promoted, young and ambitious inspector arrived at the Gorbals police office on a whim, like the proverbial new broom.'

One day, he called for the older and more experienced sergeant on his shift to come into his office.

'Willie,' he said, 'Have you ever heard of a female from the Govanhill area of Glasgow, nick-named the "Heilan' Coo"?'

The elderly sergeant thought for a moment, shook his head and said, 'Can't say I have. Why? Should I?'

'Well,' said the Inspector, 'I have it on good authority that this particular female is allegedly, allowing uniformed police officers to frequent her house in order to drink alcohol and sample her sexual favours!

'Och, I don't believe that for one minute.' replied the sergeant rather dismissively.

'Well that's what I've heard.' said the inspector. 'But we'll leave it meantime until I have something concrete to go on!'

A few weeks later, the inspector received further information relative to the inquiry he was making and this time there was an address to go with it.

He rushed into the sergeant's room and ecstatically announced.

'Quick, Willie, come with me – I've got an address to check out. I think it could be the house belonging to the Heilan' Coo.'

Both Supervisors left the office and made their way down the road on foot.

Finally, they arrived outside a large red sandstone tenement building in the Govanhill area of Glasgow.

Confirming the address written down in his notebook, he said, 'This is it!'

He appeared very excited by this news and as they both entered the close entrance, he said, 'It's on the first landing to the right Willie.'

Upstairs they went, whereby the Inspector knocked on the door.

A moment or two passed, before the door was eventually opened by a small, dirty-faced little boy, who on seeing the police officers standing there in full uniform, stood staring back at them.

Then, a female voice, with a broad South Uist accent, called out from inside the house. 'Well! Who is it William?'

Too which the small boy confidently replied, It's my uncle Willie, wi' another wan o' his pals!'

Timex Watch
• • •

My neighbours are two cute young lesbians, who asked me what I would like for my birthday. I was quite surprised, when they gave me a Timex! It was very nice of them, but I'm pretty sure that they misunderstood me, when I said: 'I just wanna watch!'

Talking Too Much!

...

Jimmy and I were away with the Traffic police football team to Edinburgh for a Scottish cup game, after which, one of the opposing team was looking for a lift into Glasgow.

'Jimmy and Harry are going your way, they'll give you a lift, won't you guys? The inspector said. Reluctantly, we agreed to his request.

All the way back, our unwanted passenger sat in the rear with his head between our front seats, talking non-stop crap.

Every now and then, whilst driving along the M8 motorway, I would look at Jimmy and make a sign with my eyes. Convinced we were on the same wavelength, I suddenly indicated and pulled onto the hard shoulder, prior to our exit road.

'What's up Harry?' Jimmy asked.

'The motor behind was flashing me. I think I might have a problem at the back of the car.'

'Do you want me to get out and check it for you?' Asked our chatty volunteer.

'Would you mate!' said Jimmy

'No problem.' At that he got out the car and as he walked to the rear of the car to check . . . I promptly drove off, leaving him behind.

Whereby, we both laughed uncontrollably all the way home!

The Polis Interpreter

· · ·

A Chinese man was apprehended and conveyed to the police station, suspected of theft and credit card fraud.

During the subsequent interview regarding the charges which he had been brought in for, the Chinese man deliberately gave the impression to the arresting officers that he could not speak or understand any words of English, although he had lived in the UK for more than twenty years.

The arresting officers were convinced their suspect was deliberately delaying proceedings and could understand and speak English fluently.

However, the duty inspector intervened and informed the arresting officers that they would require to follow police proceedings by the book and contact an interpreter for their Chinese suspect, to inform him of his legal rights, before they could proceed any further.

One of the cops then went through to the front office to call the force control room, in order to contact an interpreter to attend.

Whilst he was doing this, Gerry Docherty, a uniformed cop, approached him and asked, 'Who jailed wee Sammy Wang?'

'I did!' replied the young cop, 'but the bugger doesn't speak a word of English, so the inspector wants me to get an interpreter from Pitt Street for him.'

'Whit? Don't bother phoning Pitt Street,' said Gerry, 'I know Sammy very well – I'll interpret for him!'

'Oh, brilliant Gerry, do you speak Mandarin?' asked the young cop.

'Not really.' Gerry replied. 'But I eat a lot of Chinese grub, so I think that qualifies me to be able to speak in Sammy's language!'

Gerry then accompanied the young cop along the corridor to the interview room where Sammy was sitting. On seeing Gerry enter the room, Sammy's eyes lit up and he sat upright in his seat, whereby Gerry promptly slapped him across the head.

'So all of a sudden you don't speak English, Sammy?' asked Gerry. 'Well let's try and help you with some useful tips.' At that he gave Sammy an almighty thump, knocking him clean off his chair and as he was preparing to do so again, Sammy screamed out, 'All light! All light! I speak the f*cken Engrish, no need to take it so seliously, it was just a joke!'

Gerry then turned to the arresting cops and said, 'There ye go boys, he just needed a wee reminding that he has a perfect understanding of the Engwish language.' He then imitated Sammy. "Would you rike flied lice wiff your charge?'

As Gerry left the interview room, he was met in the corridor by the Duty Inspector who asked, 'What's all the commotion?'

'Nothing to concern you Inspector, I was just giving Sammy a crash course in English in order to save time and the added expense of an interpreter!'

This was achieved not only by Gerry's local knowledge and understanding of the language, but more importantly, knowing how to interpret and administer it properly.

Nothing to do with the police manual or, political correctness, much to the annoyance of the duty inspector.

However, Gerry added that it helps considerably, if you eat regularly in the Chinese Restaurant where Sammy works as a waiter and therefore, know him personally!!

Got A Light Mate!

• • •

Stuart Bailey was a former colleague of mine from Lanarkshire who liked a dram and a cigarette.

One evening he was standing in his local pub, prior to the No Smoking ban, having a quiet drink, and had just lit up a cigarette, when a stranger, standing at the bar next to him, holding a cigarette in his hand, asked Stuart, 'Excuse me, mate, do you have a light there please?'

Stuart, looked him straight in the eye, and replied, 'Yes I do thanks!' At that, he turned away with his back to him.

The stranger then tapped Stuart on the shoulder and asked, 'Well, do you think you could give me a light please?'

Stuart turned around to face the stranger and said, 'Naw! I'm not giving you a light! Now bugger off!'

The stranger remarked, 'There's no need to be so rude! After all, I was only asking you for a light for my cigarette!'

Stuart responded to this remark by saying, 'Is that right mate? Whit's your name?'

The stranger answered, 'It's Richard, but my friends call me Dick for short!'

'Well Dick "for short", just let me analyse your request for a moment. Now, you're asking me to give you a light for your cigarette, is that correct?'

'That's correct!' confirmed Dick.

Stuart continued with his analysis, 'Right then! So, I give you a light and you offer me a cigarette as a polite gesture and I take the cigarette off you. Next thing is, we start talking. Y'know, the usual pish! Where are you from?

I'll ask and you'll reply, "Oh, I'm from such and such a place, but I'm just up here on business," and we'll get right involved in conversation.

'Then I'll go to buy a drink for myself and I'll feel obliged to ask you if you want one and you'll say, "Yes please, Stuart, I'll have a whisky and a half-pint of lager." And while I'm getting them in, you'll give me a fag and I'll give you another light.

'Then it'll be your turn to order up the drinks and so on and so forth and we'll both end up totally pished.

'So I'll ask you how you got over here? And you'll reply, "Oh I drove over in the car, I'm staying in a hotel in Glasgow."

'Then I'll feel terrible for getting you so drunk and I'll say, "Well you cannae drive yer car like that, Dick," and I'll invite you back to my house, which is within walking distance o' the pub, for a cup o' coffee and when we get back there, my missus will take one look at your face and say to me, "Stuart! You cannae let that Dick drive a car in that condition, we better let him stay the night and sleep it off!"

'So I'll invite you to stay the night and sleep it off. But there's a slight problem with that synopsis, Dickie boy. You see, my house only has two bedrooms – the missus and I sleep in one and my innocent, gorgeous, voluptuous, seventeen-year-old daughter Britney, sleeps in the other one.

'So you, Dickie my boy, would have to get yer head down for the night on the sofa in the lounge, with the spare duvet o'er ye. And sure as shite in a wean's minging nappie, during the night, ya randy bastard, yer old hormones will start twitching and ye'll get up and go for a wander about the house, with yer aroused boaby sticking oot in front o' ye, like a divining rod, leading the way.

'Lo and behold, you'll go sneaking upstairs into my innocent, gorgeous, voluptuous, seventeen-year-old daughter Britney's bedroom for a gander at her pure lily-white, untouched body, and while she's lying there like a wee angel, in a deep sleep, ye'll slip into bed beside her and have yer evil end away!

'My innocent young virgin daughter will be totally oblivious to this and just think she's been having her first sexually explicit erotic dream during the night, having never met you.

'Next morning, the wife and I will get up out of bed and discover that you Dickie my boy have buggered off in a fast black intae Glesca afore we're even down the stairs.

'Oh aye, and another thing – my wife will be so worried about you, she'll say, "I wonder what time that Dick got up this morning?" and, "I hope that Dick had some breakfast afore he left the house?" and best of all, Dick must have been aroused early, I just hope he wasn't frozen stiff with the cold during the night?"

'Aroused? Probably. Frozen? Maybe – Stiff? Most definitely!'

'Nothing else will be said and I'll think everything in the garden is rosy. Totally unaware of course, that during the night, you have planted yer family seedlings in my daughters incubator, ya manky bastard!

'My young, innocent, gorgeous, voluptuous daughter Britney, will suddenly and without trying too hard, gather more weight than Bridget Jones! And instead o' getting ready for the school prom dance, she'll look like she's getting ready to go sumo wrestling with the Wan Hung Lo brothers!

'Then nine months down the line, guess what? We're Granny and Grandpa Bailey, to a wee Richard, call me Dick for short, who my once, innocent, gorgeous and voluptuous young daughter Britney has just dropped off at the Royal Maternity Hospital, compliments of a Mr Richard (call me Dick) Boner, who just happens to have done a Lord Lucan!'

At this point, an agitated Dick interrupted Stuart, 'I won't do that! I won't! I won't! I promise you I won't!'

Too which Stuart replied, 'Ye're fucken right ye won't! 'cause yer not getting a bloody light!'

Window Cleaners

• • •

Walking through the office one day, I answered the telephone to an irate female who reported, 'Somebody has just poured yoghurt or cream all over my bedroom window!'

On hearing her outburst, I offered her a solution: 'Well, can you not just go out and clean it off?'

The rather perturbed female caller replied, 'What?! With a disabled son?'

At which point I paused for a moment, before answering, 'I think that's a bit drastic missus, I was going to suggest using a bucket of water and a cloth!'

Guns in the Family

...

One day a telephone call was received at the CID office, from a male informant, who wished to remain anonymous.

The information was, that there were several guns within a house at . . . there was even an old-fashioned Tommy gun. The informant supplied the young detective with the address. The young detective officer, convinced that the call was genuine and keen to make a good impression, coupled with a discovery like this, arranged with other armed CID officers, to attend at the address with a warrant, to make a search of the premises for the alleged firearms.

As the CID officers made their final preparations prior to leaving the police station, David Toner, an elderly, bespectacled uniformed officer who was presently performing indoor duties as the CID office clerk, overheard the entire episode of events and entered the room with his gold rimmed half-moon glasses perched on the bridge of his nose and carrying a copy of the public Voters Roll log for the entire area, under one arm and opening it up at a page he had previously marked off, he handed it over to the eager young detective officer and said, 'Aye son, your informant was spot on, there are "Gunns" at that address, mind you, there's an entire family of them . . . Oh, and the father's name is Tommy Gunn!'

Surprise! Surprise!
· · ·

Dougie Mack was a cop with a mad passion for eating his culinary delight: pie and beans. He absolutely adored them. The only problem was, they didn't particularly agree with him.

You see, after consuming a few pints of Guinness and a few greasy pies smothered with baked beans, Dougie would suffer the most horrendous, obnoxious flatulence, in fact, he was an out-and-out 'pongo'!

Suffice to say, wherever he go, the Pongo!

Being a single bloke, this did not unduly bother him, until he met the woman of his dreams, a policewoman on another shift and started dating her.

After dating regularly for over a year, the inevitable happened, when they got engaged and subsequently hand-cuffed – sorry, I mean married. (Same thing!)

Several months later, Dougie was involved in a big drug-bust court case and, having obtained a guilty verdict, he accompanied some of his fellow drug squad mates, to a local hostelry for an afternoon bevvy session to celebrate.

After swallowing numerous pints of Guinness, Dougie the dutiful husband, made his excuses and left the celebrations to catch his bus for home.

However, whilst standing at the bus stop awaiting it's arrival, he could smell an aroma, which had escaped his nostrils and taste buds for so long – yes, it was that of pie and beans!

The aroma to his nose was the equivalent of Chanel No 5, to a woman – pure nectar from the gods. Not that you would get too many women wearing the pie and bean fragrance, but you get my drift in comparison I hope!

Anyways, as he stood there soaking up this bouquet of fragrance, he thought to himself, why not have just one?

One couldn't hurt anybody and it would go a long way to satisfying his craving!

Finally convinced, he marched into the baker's shop and purchased one.

Oh how he enjoyed it – three bites and it was gone. Suddenly it came to him that it was still quite early, so why not have another and he could walk part of the route home, ridding himself of the unwanted foul flatulence on the way, thereby, he could arrive home to his house, with his lovely wife, none the wiser.

He talked himself into it and re-entered the shop.

The greedy pig didn't stop at one and before he left the shop, he had scoffed three more. They hardly touched the sides of his throat, on their way down.

Off he went along the road, (wind-assisted) striding it out like a beat policeman, farting away, like a four-bob rocket on Guy Fawkes Night, every few minutes – 'Bbbrrrpppppp!'

It was like walking on Nike Air, without wearing the trainers, as each step he took, practically blew the backside out of his trousers. It was brilliant, with no one to bother about. He was only a threat to the local wildlife.

Finally, almost at his house, he'd passed enough wind to re-write, *The Wind in the Willows* and play the lead part in *The House at Pooh Corner*.

He had single-handedly contaminated the entire countryside with his foul waste and with time left for one more blow-out before he reached his front door.

Cocking his leg up to one side, he let rip . . . 'Bbbrrrppppppp!' Pausing for a brief moment, before minging his doorbell . . . Sorry, ringing his doorbell!!

After a few moments, his wife duly answered the door, 'Hello darling!' she said, as she leant forward placing a kiss on his cheek.

'Hello, love, he responded, stepping inside the hallway he was about to remove his jacket when his wife said, 'Stop! Close your eyes, darling, I have a nice wee surprise for you!'

Being the obedient husband, he complied with her request, whereby she then lead him by the arm along the hallway with his eyes tightly closed and into the lounge area of the house.

'Right!' she said, 'On the count of three, I want you to open your eyes?' At that she began to count, 'One, two . . .' but before she could say 'three', the house telephone started ringing.

'Stop! Don't open your eyes. Promise me you'll keep them tightly closed until I return.' she pleaded with him.

'I promise, I promise!' he replied.

On that note, his wife went off into the hallway to answer the telephone.

While awaiting her return, Dougie's stomach began to rumble with a build up of gas, which he has just got to get rid of – pronto!

He stretched his neck and cocked his ear in the direction of his wife on the telephone and hearing her engaged in conversation, he let rip once again –'Bbbrrrppppppp!'

What a rasper this was and he doesn't even have a dog that he can blame it on.

The smell was so strong you could practically taste it!

If it was canned, it could be sold as insect repellent!

There's probably enough vitamins in it, to find a cure for a Mediterranean disease!

He began blowing frantically and waving his hands about in an effort to disperse the smell and still with his eyes closed tightly.

What a good husband (probably stinging anyway) – he was totally bowfin'!

His wife called out to him from the hallway. 'I hope you still have your eyes closed tightly?'

Dougie responded by shouting back to her, 'Yes, sweetie pie!'

There was nothing sweet about this pie and he knew it, I can assure you!

'I wouldn't want to spoil your surprise for me.' He then quietly muttered to himself, 'I hope tac f*ck it's no' pie and bloody beans.'

He then giggled to himself nervously, this just happened to coincide with another rumble in his stomach – surely not again? He felt like he was about to lift off! Look out NASA, his bomb doors were about to open fully!

Was this a three-minute warning that the brownies are coming? Definitely!

However, he couldn't go to the toilet, because he would have to pass his wife in the hallway.

Panic-stricken, he had a repeat of his last fart, only double and in stereo sound, 'Bbrrrppppp – Bbrrrppppp'! – 'Uugghhhhhh!!'

It felt as though he had just passed a ten-pin bowling ball . . . whole! He is absolutely stinking!

He smells as if he is in the advanced stages of decomposing.

Local farmers would pay him, just to roll over and fertilise their fields.

The UN are searching Iraq for chemical weapons and here we have our very own located in a suburban estate in Glasgow!

This last one takes the biscuit.

This time, the bunnet is off his head and he is vigorously waving it about in front and behind him, in an effort to dilute the stench that he has produced with the room's scented atmosphere.

Then panic took over as his wife finished off her telephone conversation.

He stopped his frantic waving and tried to act natural as his wife re-entered the room and said, 'Right, did you open your eyes?'

'No darling, I did not.' he replied. 'Honest!'

'Good!' she said. 'Well, you can open them now!'

Very slowly, he opened his eyes and gasped in horror! As, seated around the room, were police colleagues, friends and relatives, who in unison, burst into song,

'Happy Birthday to You, Happy Birthday to You!' Aaaarrrrgggghhhhh!!!!

Lucky Tatties

. . .

I was recently reminiscing with my brother Allan about sweets we used to buy, like MB Bars, Whoppas, Milk Dainties, etc and we brought up the subject of Lucky Tatties or Lucky Potatoes, depending where you were brought up.

Now, for those not old enough to know what a Lucky Tattie was, let me explain that it was a brick hard, flat brown thing, covered with brown cinnamon powder, which you had to bite through and try and chew in order to eventually find, concealed inside the centre of it, a key ring, a glass marble (jorry) or some other ridiculous little toy.

For me, the 'Lucky' part was that you didn't break your teeth while trying to bite it or, swallow the article inside it and choke to death!

Another piece of food we used to eat regularly was my auld Granny's, home-made clootie dumpling, made in a pillow case.

It was absolutely brilliant, but for some reason, and best known to her generation, when mixing the ingredients to make it, she would add some silver threepenny coins to the mixture. These were coins the size of a 5 pence piece. Now what was that all about?

In one portion alone, I bit into three. Mind you, I swallowed two of them. Everybody would say, 'Away ye go ya lucky wee bugger!'

'Lucky?' My Granny just tried to choke me by putting coins in my slice of dumpling and I'm 'Lucky'! Don't think so mate! Imagine if one of them stuck in yer gullet? There's no way the 'change' would do you any good!

And I also had the added embarrassment of having to check my 'stools' for the next few days until I passed them and even then, I had to swallow several spoonfuls of liquid paraffin and stand well clear, as they came out fast and hard, they nearly cracked the toilet pan.

To crown it all, when I told my mother what I had just passed, she took them off me.

'Lucky!' 'Lucky my arse!'

A Clash of Personalities

• • •

I'd just arrived for duty when I was summoned to the chief inspector's office for my annual appraisal/assessment, often referred to as your MOT.

Halfway through the appraisal report, the chief inspector said, 'I detect from some of the remarks made by your shift sergeant that you don't get on with him?'

'I think that's a fair observation', I replied.

'So what appears to be the problem?' he asked me.

'It's just a clash of personalities, sir.' I said. 'He doesn't have one!'

'A personality clash?' he asked before continuing. 'Do you think a change of shift would help?'

Whereupon I replied with a straight face, 'Frankly, between you and me sir, I'd have to say no! I don't think he could get on with anybody!'

That's My Dad!

* * *

I was writing a wee story about my late father the other day and by pure accident, I came across some interesting facts that I was unaware of, so let me tell you them first.

At the age of thirteen, having left school, he worked as a motorbike dispatch rider for the fire brigade and by the age of sixteen, two years into World War 2 and desperate to serve his country, he enrolled in the Royal Navy.

Due to being very tall for his age, he easily passed for eighteen years old and was accepted, no questions asked.

Several convoys later, at the end of the war, he was accepted back into the fire brigade full time, having failed the medical for the police, because he had flat feet!

Accepted by the fire brigade, he was to become the youngest fireman in Britain and had the distinction of having served his country and been awarded six medals as a result. Something that a lot of his older colleagues in the brigade had never done!

He also continued to serve in the armed forces, by enlisting in the Royal Navy Volunteer Reserves, and when he was required to resign years later due to a back injury, he found it hard to accept. So, as soon as he recovered, he contacted the Royal Engineers Territorial Army Reserves and enlisted with them, serving for a further twelve years.

He was also very much a Royalist during this time and would never tolerate anyone talking badly about them, or any part of the Armed Forces, and when I say, 'he didn't tolerate anyone berating them', I mean to the extent where he would have no hesitation in resorting to physical assault!

Now with this in mind, I will now relate an incident that took place one evening in a pub in Glasgow, while he and I were sitting having a quiet drink, whilst awaiting the arrival of one of his ex-army buddies.

We had been sitting at a table in the middle of the lounge for about half an hour, when in walked his old mate Cameron.

During the preceding conversation, Cameron intimated that he had arranged with his daughters fiancé, a newspaper reporter, to join us for a casual drink.

In the interim period, before he arrived, they were talking about the latest news regarding two young army squaddies, who had been killed whilst on duty, and how tragic it had been, when the door of the pub opened and in came Cameron's future son-in-law, the reporter.

He joined us at the table and after the polite introductions I went to the bar to fetch some drinks.

On my return to the table, they were discussing the situation regarding the young soldiers, and the reporter said that he was doing an article on them and that's why he was late in arriving.

My father then remarked that it was sad to hear about the loss of life of two young soldiers who were 'pawns', placed in a situation they would rather not have been in.

Whereby the reporter replied flippantly, 'They get well paid to be there, so they know what they're doing when they join up, and dying for their Queen and country, is just part of the game!'

Within a very short space of time, the situation was becoming very heated and I immediately feared the worst for the smug reporter's boyish good looks, for I could visibly see the hackles beginning to rise in my father's neck as he pointed out that, 'They were only young boys, who were sent over to another country to save lives by keeping both sides apart and thereby maintaining peace.'

However, the reporter was having none of it and replied with a short, sharp and resounding, 'Tough! That's life.'

The word 'Tough' had barely left his lips, and I doubt very much if he saw it coming, or remembers much about it afterwards, but it coincided with my father's big fist coming the opposite way, directly across the table and connecting full on with the reporters face, knocking him clean off his seat and sending him sprawling across the floor, whereby he landed flat out on his back, about ten feet away, totally unconscious!

Cameron did not appear to be the least bit surprised at the outcome of the heated discussion between his daughter's fiancé and my father, as he signalled for me to get my father out of the pub quickly, while he attempted to try and bring him round.

Along with my father, we left the premises and stopped a taxi to take us home, although I did encounter some resistance from my father, who wanted to remain there and finish off his drink.

About an hour after we had arrived back at his house, when the phone rang and I answered it. It was Cameron.

I immediately made to apologise for my father's behaviour towards his future son-in-law, but Cameron interrupted me in mid-sentence.

'Are ye kidding? Fu*k him! I knew he couldnae keep his big mouth shut. That's why I invited him to come along. He was bound to say something during the night about the army or the navy, and knowing yer auld man, it was only a matter of time, but I didnae expect the big man to react so quickly. What a 'dull yin' he gave him. He's been sparkled ever since!'

On hearing this, I had to ask Cameron.

'So why invite him along if you knew that he would say something that would upset my dad and end up like it did?'

'Cause I cannae stand the prick, but I couldnae dae anything myself! He's been dating my daughter for a while noo, but he's bad news, pardon the pun. He's a cheeky arrogant bastard and I don't like him one bit. But my daughter disnae see it and refuses to listen to me.

'Listen Harry, I've been in your old man's company long enough to know how he reacts to anybody making remarks about the forces, and I also knew this bastard widnae be able to bite his tongue once they started talking. He's a reporter after aw, cannae keep his big mouth shut, but he'll maybe no' be able tae open it for a few weeks after that punch!

'By the way! He didnae remember a bloody thing about what happened tonight!' Cameron paused before adding, 'He's some man big Freddie, you don't mess about with him.'

So in effect, he had orchestrated the entire event, knowing my father would not be unable to sit and listen to someone bad mouthing the armed forces, without taking action against them.

However, I'm glad to report that it backfired on Cameron, when his daughter announced she was pregnant, and it didnae need to be front page news to guess who the father was!

Now, he had a future son-in-law who couldn't keep his mouth shut and a pregnant daughter, who couldn't keep her legs shut!

Sounds like the perfect couple to me!

The Job's Fucked!

· · ·

A regular saying that was regularly uttered by the many disgruntled City of Glasgow police officers during the early seventies was: 'The job's fucked.'

Every other week, a police officer, using the all-systems radio airways, would interrupt the occasional silence, by broadcasting to all mobile and radio stations, the immortal words, 'The job's fucked!'

One particular day, an assistant chief constable was visiting the HQ radio control room, when over the radio came the aforesaid broadcast, 'The job's fucked!'

The assistant chief constable, on hearing this derogatory announcement, immediately picked up the radio handset and broadcast a response, 'Would the station whom has just transmitted the last statement, please identify yourself?'

The same male voice replied, 'What for? The job's fucked!'

Getting frustrated by this anonymous caller and his remark on air, the assistant chief constable again broadcast, but this time, he identified himself over the radio.

'This is Assistant Chief Constable Bennie, would the officer who transmitted that last statement, please identify himself to me?'

To which the caller paused for a moment before replying in a droll voice, 'It's no' that fucked!'

The Wembley Weekend

. . .

One of the great week-end trips away with the police was to the international football matches between the 'Auld Enemy' – England and Scotland.

Every second year, we would pay up our money to the Police Social Club Committee, to book your seat on the bus bound for Wembley.

We would all meet up at the Lochinch Police Club, in the Pollok Estate, where we would enjoy several drinks beforehand, in order to relax us for our long bus trip.

The committee members would then call out your name and hand you an envelope with the money you had saved for the trip along with a paper carrier bag containing a half bottle of your favourite tipple and four cans of beer, for the journey.

Peter McMillan, our Committee Leader would check our names with his list, as we each in turn entered the bus.

Within minutes we were off along the Country Park leading to the main road.

Halfway along the road, Jimmy Clark would start the wind up, 'Ho Peter! Can ye get the driver tae stop. I'm needing a wee single fish?'

'Could ye no' have gone like everybody else afore we left the clubhouse?'

'I'm sorry Peter. I've got a wee bit o' a weak bladder.'

Peter went up to the driver,

'Sorry Don, but can you pull in and let one of the guys off for a pee.'

The driver pulled up and there was a mass exodus, as half the bus got off for the toilet, Peter included.

All aboard, once again and we're off.

We had only just turned onto the main road, when Davy Bell shouts out the window.

'Ho darling! Do you and yer wee pal wi' the tartan coat on fancy a trip to Wembley?'

'Cut that out Davy Bell and sit down.' Blasted Peter. 'She's just a wee woman out for a walk with her dog!'

'She might be just a dug tae you, bye the way! But I've been out wi' uglier lookin' women.'

Clarky and I immediately confirmed that – having been to several of his engagement parties.

'Och behave yersel' and sit down on yer seat you two.'

Peter decided it was time for the big speech and asked the driver to switch on the hand held microphone.

'Testing! Testing! One, Two. One, Two. Can everybody hear at the back of the bus?'

Jimmy called out, 'Aye, me Peter. I'll have a beer and so will Harry!'

'I didn't ask if ye wanted a beer! I asked if you could hear?

'Aw right! Well, Naw, I cannae hear you!' Jimmy responded.

'Would you try and be serious for a minute until I speak.' (He pauses) 'Right! I just want to remind each and everyone of you that you're representing Strathclyde Police. So at all times, I would expect you to be on your best behaviour.

'If anybody needs the toilet, we have a makeshift one at the rear, in the shape of two army jerry cans, so make sure you aim right and try not to make a mess. In the event of an accident, there's also a bucket and a mop!

'Now that's all I'm going to say on the matter, so I hope each and every one of you has a good time, thank you!'

'Okay Peter, now sit on yer arse and gie us peace!' I shouted.

As the bus joins the M74 Motorway, we are well on our way.

After several hours of continual drinking, a voice called out, 'Has anybody got a spare carrier bag or something? Big Davy Bell is goin' tae be Moby Dick.'

'Him! Goin' tae be sick? I don't think so,' said Jimmy. 'He's too tight tae part wi' anything!'

'Here, give him that one.' I said, handing one over.

Not a moment too soon as Davy buried his head in it and spewed into the bag, filling it.

Unfortunately for him, I forgot to mention it was burst at the bottom and the contents from his stomach, poured all over his trouser legs, via the hole.

Emergency procedures were required.

So we covered him up with his own jacket and told him to lie down and sleep it off, it will be alright in the morning.

Then we moved as far away from him as possible, so that the blue- bottle flies wouldn't annoy us.

Several hours later, having crossed the border into England several miles back, Don the driver pulled into a service station for a packet of cigarettes and a short break.

This was also the cue for everybody who was still awake to get off the bus and stretch their legs.

The service station was extremely busy, with football supporters from both sides, all on their way to converge on Wembley.

As Jimmy and I were walking into the shop, we were confronted by some English supporters desperate to buy some diesel, due to the fuel strike.

'Hey Jock! You don't have any spare diesel on your bus? They've ran out of it in here, due to the shortage and we're almost running on empty!'

I looked at Jimmy and he looked at me, then together we said, 'As a matter of fact, we do!' Then Jimmy adds, 'But we can only give you two. They're full jerry cans, so you'll have plenty to get you there!'

'How much do you want for them?' He asked.

'Twenty quid each.' I said.

'You're on!' Replied our new English 'buddies'.

At that point, Jimmy and I returned to the bus and I went inside and casually opened the rear emergency exit door and handed the jerry cans out to him.

'Where are you going with them?' Asked Don the driver.

'What these? Responded Jimmy. They're full to the brim wi' pish Don, so Harry and me are just going to empty them out!'

We then proceeded to humph them over to our English 'buddies' and the swap took place, for the agreed forty pounds cash.

They were ever so grateful, they even gave us a can of beer each. Little did they know, that they were taking the 'piss', so to speak!

I can visualise Mel Gibson in *Braveheart* saying, 'You can take our piss, but you'll never take our diesel!'

We promptly made our way back onto the bus and within minutes, we are back on the busy motorway, heading for our destination of Epping Forrest Hotel, some forty pounds cash better off and ten gallons of piss lighter!

However, not satisfied with the price, Jimmy felt we sold it too cheaply.

For some reason, in convincing them that it was really diesel, he had also convinced himself they were worth more! Daft bugger!

The only problem we faced now was explaining to Peter the disappearance of the jerry cans, when anyone needed to go.

'Oh shit! The jerry cans. We've left them outside the toilets at the service station and forgot to collect them on the way out.' Jimmy said convincingly.

'You'll just have to hold it in until the next stop then!' Ordered Peter.

Time for a bit of shut-eye, to prevent any more questions during the remaining part of our journey.

On arrival at our destination, Peter decided to reiterate his earlier speech about our behaviour while we were there,

'Now remember, each and everyone of you has the responsibility on your shoulders of representing Strathclyde Police, so don't be the one to let the side down!'

With these few words, we all trooped off the bus into the hotel, where we were allocated our rooms.

After some breakfast and a few beers later, Jimmy and I went up to our room to sort out our luggage.

Jimmy looked out the bedroom window and said, 'Quick Harry, check this out!'

As we both looked out across the road, there was Peter, standing outside the pub, holding himself up with a lamp-post, being sick onto the roadway.

I couldn't resist the moment and opened the window and shouted across at him,

'Hey Peter, don't hold back there! Remember you are representing Strathclyde Police.'

Before he could look up and focus on where it came from, I had closed the window and curtains.

The following day, everyone was up early and all decked out in their tartan kilts and me, dressed like Les Mckeown, in my Bay City Rollers trousers and shirt, oh and a few of them wore the obligatory 'See You Jimmy' red wig.

How common! . . . I managed to sell mine!

Down at reception waiting for us, were a few ex-pats, who had also arrived for the big game, along with a female, who turned out to be a cousin of one of our lot.

She introduced herself to us as 'Ester' and there was no simple 'peck' on the cheek from this 'burd', when introducing herself, it was legs wrapped around you and tongue down the throat stuff.

I instantly dubbed her, 'Ester the Molester'!

En-route to the Wembley Way, we were informed that there was a public transport strike and therefore, we would have to walk part of the way.

Walking along the route, we came across the Prince of Wales pub. Mind you, that was not much of a surprise, 'cause there was one on almost every street corner. He must be doing really well!

'Let's go in here for a pint.' Was the cry from Jimmy, as we all trooped in.

After several beers, followed by some whisky chasers, I made my way to the toilet.

As I stood there decked out in my Bay City Roller's gear, tartan rosette, tartan beret and the Saltire painted on both cheeks (of my face, I should add). All very colourful.

Suddenly, the door of the toilet opened and in came this six feet plus, mean looking black guy, wearing a long black leather coat to the floor, with lemon coloured fedora-style hat and long feather, lemon trousers, a lemon shirt and a pair of lemon shoes.

I thought to myself, I've stumbled across Big Bird from *Sesame Street*!

As he stood at the cubicle next to me, looking me up and down, he allowed himself a smile, 'What-choo wearing der man?' He asked me, as he giggled.

I looked him up and down for a moment, then said, 'Who's a pretty boy! . . . What am I wearing? Check yersel' out big man. Yer done up like a big yellow canary! I suppose ye sing as well?'

I then looked down at him, while in full flow and said, 'Now there's another myth about you black guys . . . Eh?'

He stood looking at me, completely flummoxed by the accent, as I nonchalantly left him alone in the toilet to try and work it out.

I re-joined the rest of the guys and after a quick rendition of 'Shang-a-Lang', we left to continue on our merry way to Wembley.

As things turned out, it wasn't a good day for Scotland.

For a start the England team showed up and promptly thumped us 5-1. But in all fairness to Scotland, up until they scored the first goal, we were actually drawing with them!

So that was twice the English took the pish out of us in the space of two days! If you get my drift.

However, back at the hotel, the 'commiseration' party was in full swing on our return. The booze was flowing.

Ester the Molester was on the sofa, wrapped around two guys like a python, probing the ear of one of them with her big horrible tongue.

The lounge area was littered with carry-out pizza, kebabs and fish suppers, as the drink flowed relentlessly with not a penny changing hands.

All the kitchen staff had locked up the fridges and left for the evening, leaving us more or less to fend for ourselves, hence the discarded carry-out meals.

As the evening progressed, the bar staff were the next to disappear and it was now being run by Peter and Willie from the committee, who seemed more at home, pulling the pints, as opposed to pulling the burds. Which was a first for them.

I quickly went upstairs to change and as I walked into the room, I couldn't help but notice there was someone sleeping in our beds.

Clarky appeared from the toilet, as if nothing was wrong, so I said to him, while putting my arm around his neck to whisper,

'Jimmy! Someone is sleeping in my bed and I have just noticed, someone is sleeping in your bed also. Now I know for a fact it's not me, you, or Goldilocks, so gonny tell me who the fuck it is?'

'So you've noticed then?' He said, sounding surprised and totally cool.

'Yes, I've noticed?' I said. 'And so would Stevie Wonder have spotted the beards, they're no' exactly invisible. So who is it?'

'It's just big Rab Hagen and his mate. They just needed somewhere to crash out for a couple of hours, but I've told them that afterwards, they'll have to sleep on the floor!'

'The floor, maybe! The corridor, most definitely!' I argued.

As it was, they both awoke and after a few moments, they decided to join us down stairs in the bar with the rest of the rabble for a drink.

The party was still in full swing with no obvious sign that it was about to slow down any and we were now joined by the 'Old Bill', who had their helmets and tunics off, sitting back enjoying the mood and being offered the odd whisky. In a pint glass!

Ester the Molester had somehow managed to get herself hand-cuffed to the police sergeant, who thought it was a good laugh.

Her idea, not his and her tongue, which appeared to grow like an erection every time she stuck it out, was investigating his tonsils and beyond!

The fun atmosphere amongst our group and the many visitors who had decided to join our party, continued long into the night.

Eventually, as the party started to break up, big Wullie Smith and the young probationer cop, were performing a taxi service and driving some of the locals home, in the police Panda car.

Wullie had recently passed his Police Advanced Driving Course and was tutoring the young probationer, whilst his sergeant was presently 'tied up', or should I say 'engaged' with Ester!

Unfortunately, on his return to the hotel, the young cop attempted to take a bend too fast and careered across the road and through a brick wall, before coming to rest in a front garden. Not exactly as planned.

Due to the young man not having a driving licence, big Wullie did the honorable thing (no he didn't take the blame.)

He legged it away from the locus, along with the young cop, back to the hotel!

On his return, The police sergeant, with the aid of Ester the Molester and a few others had managed to remove most of his own clothing and was now lying half naked, asleep in the lounge area.

His tunic, helmet, epaulettes, shirt, tie, whistle and truncheon, were all gone. Only his hand-cuffs were visible, because they were still attached to his ankles and the table.

What a job I had fitting his metropolitan helmet into my case! Although Jimmy said, 'Where's Patricia when you need her. She could have packed that helmet in there nae bother!'

The following morning, when we went downstairs for breakfast, the bombsite we had left had been cleared. Not a trace of anything!

After our breakfast, we congregated outside at the bus, in order to load our luggage and head back up the road for Scotland.

While standing there waiting, Peter arrived to inform us that Don the driver was missing and he required some help to look for him.

During the search, I suggested we load up our luggage into the back area of the bus.

Lo and behold, when I lifted up the door, there was Don the driver, lying flat out, in a drunken stupor alongside Ester the Molester, wrapped tightly around him like a sleeping bag!

We quickly called off the search, dispensed with the services of Ester and began our long journey home.

With big Wullie being nominated by Clarky to drive the bus, due to Don the driver, still lying in an unconscious state!

As an Epilogue to the week-end, the hotel management sent a letter to the committee saying that, 'Strathclyde Police were welcome back anytime', due to their 'impeccable behaviour!'

Roll on the next Wembley Trip' and another encounter with the 'Auld Enemy'!

Lucky Me!
• • •

During an Old Firm football match in Glasgow, a drunken fan was shouting and gesticulating abuse at my colleague and me.

When we went towards him, he ran off across the busy main road without looking and was promptly blootered by a bus.

As I went to his assistance, he looked up at me, unfazed, and said, 'Wiz ah no' lucky I didnae hurt myself there?'

'Not really son!' I replied, as we promptly arrested him!

He'll Go Nuts!

. . .

During my refreshment period at work, one of the other cops on my shift produced a bag of nuts from his food locker, which he added into his breakfast cereal.

'What kind of nuts are they?' I asked him.

'Almonds!' he replied. 'The wife was given them as a present, from one of the old men she looks after.'

Now, to let you understand, this particular police officer's wife worked as a care assistant to the elderly and made regular visitations to their homes.

However, with this in mind, I had occasion to speak with his wife at a police function.

During the conversation, I was saying to her about how healthy her husband eats, with his fruit and nuts, especially the almonds. And I suggested, she speak to some of her elderly clients and talk them into buying walnuts and hazelnuts and give some to me, for a change.

She appeared to blush slightly, before saying, 'Do you know the full story, behind the almonds?'

Unaware of what she was talking about, I shook my head.

She then confided in me, (I love it!) and related the following story, which she made me swear, I'd keep to myself!

Apparently, while she visiting one of her elderly patients, he had asked her if she liked almond nuts. She stated she didn't, but her husband was very fond of them.

At that, the elderly patient presented her with a glass jar, filled to the brim with almonds, to give to him.

Delighted by the old man's kind gesture, the cop had tucked into them, munching away while watching TV, crushing them over his breakfast cereal, adding them to his home made Indian curry meal, in fact, just about anything you could add nuts too, he added them.

The following week, on returning to the elderly patient on her routine visit, she handed him a large Galaxy chocolate bar as a thank you for the jar of almonds.

The old man thanked her kindly and producing a full jar of sugared almonds, he said, 'I'll give you this jar as well, once I have sooked all the sugar icing off them!!'

YUCK!!

Hearing Things

· · ·

A ned in the sheriff court in Glasgow was being sentenced for his offence and was asked by the sheriff.

'Have you anything you would like to say?'

The accused replied rather despondently, 'Fuck all!'

The sheriff called out to the procurator fiscal, 'What did he just say there?'

'Fuck all! m'lord!' replied the Fiscal.

To which the sheriff said, 'I'm sure I saw his lips move!'

The Truth, The Whole Truth

• • •

As a young newly appointed police officer, I was cited to attend the Sheriff Court for the first time, in order to give evidence for the prosecution in a trial involving a breach of the peace.

I was very nervous as I stood in the witness box being asked questions by the procurator fiscal. During my evidence, I stated that the accused had been bawling, shouting, cursing and swearing in a public place.

The procurator fiscal asked me to tell the court what they had actually shouted during the disturbance.

Nervously, I replied, 'They were shouting that the police were a bunch of "effen bees", sir!'

'Yes constable, I appreciate what you are saying and realise that you are trying to spare our blushes, but I need you to tell the court the exact words they used,' explained the fiscal.

'They used swear words at us sir,' I replied.

'Yes, I'm well aware of that constable, but what I would like you to tell the court today, is the actual words the accused used toward you when they swore.'

The procurator fiscal, was by now becoming exasperated by my inexperience. So I took a deep breath and blurted out, 'They shouted that we were a bunch of . . . "Fucken Bastards" sir.'

'Thank you for that!' responded the procurator fiscal before continuing. 'And did you apprehend them?'

To which I replied without any hesitation, 'You're fucken right I did!'

I'll Tell Him Tomorrow, Maybe!
• • •

One evening, a well-dressed male accountant picked up a young female prostitute from the red-light district of Blythswood Square in Glasgow.

Having agreed to a price for full sex, he drove off with her in his car, to her home address, on the Southside of the City.

They both stripped off and engaged in sexual intercourse, after which, while the female was in the toilet washing, the accountant got dressed and quickly left the house, neglecting to pay the prostitute the agreed fee for the services she had provided.

Not to be outdone so easily, the aggrieved female contacted her minder, who just happened to be in the nearby vicinity.

Armed with a baseball bat, the minder confronted the accountant as he made his way out of the high-rise tower block, en-route to his parked car.

The accountant, displayed some wonderful athleticism and ran like hell, pursued by Babe Ruth, armed with the baseball bat.

At this point an anonymous call was made to the police station, regarding one male being pursued by another male, armed with a large stick.

I was immediately dispatched to attend the call, whereby, on my arrival, I observed and apprehended Babe Ruth. After hand-cuffing him, I placed him in the rear of the police car, while I obtained a full statement about the incident from the visibly shaking accountant.

Whilst noting the statement, I was beckoned over by a young woman in the large assembled crowd. It was the young prostitute who had been involved and she proceeded to relate her side of the story with regards to the events that had taken place earlier in the evening.

Having been made aware of this new information, I returned to the accountant, who immediately blurted out, 'Whatever she said, she's lying, she's a lying little whore!'

I then informed him of the story related to me by the young female and asked for his comments. The smug accountant freely admitted giving her a lift home because she had looked unwell, but strenuously denied being involved with her in any sexual act. In fact, he went as far to say, 'I did not have sexual relations with that woman.'

(Where have I heard that line before Bill?)

'She's a lying little whore, but then, what do you expect from the residents about this area?' he replied condescendingly.

I said, facetiously, 'You're right enough sir, who ever heard of an accountant cheating a client out of their money!' I then paused for a moment before continuing, 'Anyway, sir, I have to ask you a personal question here! Do you definitely deny having had sexual intercourse with this girl?'

'I certainly do! What do you take me for? I'm a happily married man.' The accountant responded with his pitiful denial.

'Well sir!' I replied. 'I'm ever so glad to hear you say that, because apparently she's been diagnosed HIV positive and she continues to entertain men in her house for unprotected sexual intercourse!'

On hearing this, the accountant's facial expression changed dramatically, as the colour visibly drained from his face and he became unsteady on his feet.

'Are you OK sir?' I asked him. 'You look as if you're going to faint!'

The accountant replied very quietly, 'Not really! I'm feeling a bit nauseous and would like to go home to my wife and family now!'

'But what about Babe Ruth with the baseball bat? We haven't charged him yet?' I said.

The accountant replied, 'I'm not interested. I'd like to drop all the charges against him and go home please, I'm not feeling very well with all this going on!'

'I'm not surprised, sir, but are you sure, because he looked really nasty with that big baseball bat?' I remarked facetiously.

'Yes I'm positive, now can I just go home please? I've wasted enough time here.' the accountant said.

'Not a problem, sir. Just sign my notebook to the effect that you don't want to proceed with the charges!' I said. 'That way, there's no harm done, so by all means, you can go on your way now!'

The accountant then walked off rather unsteadily to his car before getting in and driving off.

'You might have told him you were only kidding about the HIV stuff!' responded my colleague.

To which I replied, 'What for? You heard him give the Bill Clinton speech – "I did not have sexual relations with that woman!"'

Now why would I disbelieve the lying, cheating, adulterous bastard!'

PS. If you're the accountant involved and reading this, remove that rope from around your neck. I was only a joking!

No Armchair Stampede

· · ·

There had been an incident, at the rear of Celtic Football Park in Glasgow, whereby, it was alleged, that Strathclyde Police mounted officers, had deliberately stampeded, football supporters who had congregated in the area of Janefield Street, Glasgow.

This sensitive police enquiry was being investigated by one of our most senior and respected officers, Chief Superintendent John T. Dickson.

During this ongoing enquiry, there was an international football match coming up, between Scotland and England at Hampden Park and I was desperately trying to get tickets for it.

This particular day, I was called into Superintendent Jim Irwin's office and he said to me, 'I've to ask you, Harry, are you still looking for tickets for the big game? If so, Mr Dickson has two for sale.'

Having replied that I was looking for tickets, he called Mr Dickson at his office in Pitt Steet HQ, to inform him.

'Right Harry!' said the superintendent. 'You've to go up to his office right now and collect them!'

I went straight to HQ and knocked on the chief superintendent's office door.

'In you come, Harry!' he shouted, then he opened a drawer and taking out the match tickets, he handed them over to me.

'Don't you fancy it sir?' I asked.

'Yes, of course! But nowadays I prefer to watch the game in the comfort of my armchair in the house!' he said convincingly.

To which I couldn't resist replying, jokingly of course, 'Well, let's be honest, sir, you've less chance of getting trampled by a big bloody polis horse!'

Needless to say he was not amused by my comment. But I bet he had a right good chuckle after I left his office!

Elvis Lives

. . .

After his umpteenth road accident whilst driving another police car, a certain police officer was transferred from mobile patrol, to assisting the station counter staff.

His fellow officers, had cruelly dubbed him, 'Elvis', because, he had more hits than the Beatles.

Whilst I was over at the office with a prisoner, Elvis was working at the charge bar, processing the prisoners, by means of the computer.

I asked him if he was enjoying working at a computer?

Without pausing or lifting his head, 'Elvis replied facetiously. 'Put it this way, I must be doing okay – I haven't crashed it . . . *YET!*'

Ladies and Gentlemen
– Ben Doon

• • •

Whilst a member of the Police Social Committee, it was your duty from time to time to act as the master of ceremony for the night at a cabaret function being held in the club.

Up until then, I had always managed to avoid it but, with the absence of some of the members, I was nominated to take my turn.

The star of the cabaret was a very funny Scottish comedian, called Ben Gunn, whom I was introduced to on his arrival at the club earlier in the evening.

He gave me this spiel that he wanted me to say in my introduction, about how he had just returned from a very successful tour of America and was now appearing as top of the bill on the Sidney Devine Silver Jubilee Show, being held at the Pavillion Theatre, in Glasgow.

'After the performance', he said, 'we'll have a drink!'

Now, earlier in the evening, this would not have been a problem but, after several large Whyte & MacKay whiskies, the art of breathing was becoming a big problem for me.

It came to the penultimate act, a Caribbean steel band, dressed in bright orange shirts. They looked like they had all been Tangoed as they played their big oil drums.

By the way, the nearest they came to the Caribbean, was in a holiday brochure, because I knew three out of four of them personally, having recognised them as drivers on the corporation buses, working out of the Larkfield bus garage in Glasgow.

With the previous turn, a country and western act called the Pheasant Pluckers, I had developed dyslexia and read their introduction wrong referring to them, as some 'C***s with vests on,' and, 'They're Pleasant F*****s.'

The other committee members put it down to nerves and were telling me, 'Right Harry, we think you got away with that one, but don't make any mistakes with the introduction of Ben!'

I jumped on to the stage with my microphone and said confidently, 'Let's hear you one more time – all the way from Jamaica (Street), the Govanhill Caribbean Steel Band!'

The assembled audience applauded enthusiastically.

As the applause died down I said, 'They rejected an engagement to go on a worldwide tour. Apparently two of the band members wanted to go somewhere else! I'm also informed that the boys want me to tell you, they're sorry there will be no encores as there's a shortage of bus drivers tonight and they've all got to report for double shifts!'

I continued in this vein, getting carried away with myself, leaning on the microphone stand like a real pro.

'Two of the band members are actual twins! They used to be triplets but they ate the other brother between them one night! In true conundrum fashion, he was ate before he was seven!'

Just at that, a committee member from the side of the stage whispered loudly, 'Get on with it Harry.'

'Now! We have come to the star of our show, an act that has been thrown off more stages than big John Wayne! In fact, he was telling me he is just back from America, where he underwent a nose transplant, but unfortunately, his finger rejected it!'

Suddenly, through the smokey haze I could see some of the committee members making their way down the sides of the hall, trying not to draw too much attention to themselves, but I was on a roll and wasn't going to get off the stage that easily, so I continued, 'He was also telling me earlier that while he was in America for three weeks, he lost 9 stones of ugly fat – apparently he got a quickie divorce!'

That was the last straw – one of the committee had the other end of the microphone and was pulling and tugging it, so in order to prevent any further embarrassment, I quickly announced, 'So will you please put your hands together and give a big Lochinch Police Club welcome to the one and only Mr Ben Doon! Hic!'

Ben was not one bit amused at my introduction. He took the mike off me and called me a frustrated comedian.

He then did his performance, cutting his cabaret act short by twenty minutes and promptly left the club.

Needless to say, I was never again asked to perform as the MC at a police social club! I did apologise to Ben when we met on another occasion! But I think he still held a grudge!

The Spark-le is Still There

. . .

After twenty-five years of marriage, a police inspector surprised his wife by returning with her to the hotel, where they had spent their first honeymoon night.

The following day, the inspector drove her to an area where a beautiful big oak tree stood, near to a farmer's field. This was where they had enjoyed their first romantic kiss!

They both got out of the car and hand-in-hand, they walked over to the special spot.

He took her in his arms and leaned her against the fence and kissed her ever so passionately.

The wife suddenly responded in an erotic manner, digging her nails into his back, gripping him tightly and biting his face.

She then jumped up on him and wrapped her legs tightly around his waist, squeezing him as she yelled and squealed ecstatically.

The inspector's reaction was one of total sexual excitement: 'Woah, darling, you were never aroused like this twenty-five years ago!'

To which his wife replied, 'No, and the farmers fence wasn't electrified then either!'

Relief, For My Relief!

...

One evening, at the completion of my shift, I was attending a friend's house to view a live boxing match and had arranged for another friend of mine also going, to call at the police station at the end of my duties so that we could share a taxi.

Now, my good friend Brad, is a six-feet-plus black guy who just happens to be a deaf mute!

Anyway, he duly arrived at my front office at the agreed time and I informed him, using sign language, that I was just awaiting my relief station officer to arrive, before I could leave, but, in the meantime, to just wait in the front office area.

Brad nodded his head that he understood and decided while waiting there to view some of the various posters of information, on the wall display.

After a few moments, the front door to the office opened.

Brad immediately felt the draught from the door on his neck and turned around to face it, as in walked Donnie, my police colleague.

With Donnie looking at me behind the office counter and Brad with his back to me, looking at Donnie, I spoke in a loud voice and said, 'For the last time, sir, there is only one officer working in this station called Donnie and I can assure you he hasn't been sleeping with your wife and daughter. Now will you fuck off out of the police station?'

All the time I was talking, Brad had his back to me, staring at Donnie, who had physically frozen in his tracks and was now staring back at Brad, with what can only be described as a look of total shock on his face that now lacked any colour.

Everything stopped for a moment while Donnie suffered in silence, then I allowed a huge grin to cover my face and said, 'Don't look so worried Donnie, it's a joke, he can't hear a word – he's totally deaf!'

At which point Donnie heaved a huge sigh of relief, before scurrying off to the toilet to relieve himself! No doubt!

Blowing Your Own Trumpet

• • •

Several years ago, the Strathclyde Police Federation, held a meeting with their counterparts, the Royal Ulster Constabulary, whereby the Irish officers, treated the Strathclyde members, to a slap-up dinner followed by a cabaret.

As they took their seats along the front of the stage, Willie Irwin, who was the Strathclyde Federation Secretary and had a fairly big nose, coupled with a dashing Clark Gable lookalike moustache, positioned himself at the centre of the delegation.

Halfway through the show, it was the turn of an Irish comedian to perform for them. After a few jokes, the comedian, looked at Willie, sitting at the front of the stage, and with a puzzled expression he said, 'Here big man, you must be really proud of that nose you have there, I mean, why else would you want to underline it?'

A Midge's Dick!

· · ·

Tommy Payne and I, dealt with a serious assault, whereby a young male was struck on the face, with a knife.

We obtained statements from witnesses, including the hospital doctor, who treated the victim's wound and a short time later, we arrested the person responsible for this vicious assault.

Months later, I received a citation to attend the Sheriff Court as a witness in the case for the prosecution.

Tommy called me and said he would attend at the registry in the police station and obtain the necessary witness statements required for the court case.

At the court, prior to the case being called, I was reading over my statement, in order to familiarise myself with the incident reported.

'What did the doctor at the hospital say about the victim's injuries?' I asked Tommy, while thumbing my way through the witness statements.

Tommy casually replied, 'The Doc stated, he was a midge's dick away from losing his eye!'

'A midge's dick? That close eh!' I said, shaking my head 'A midge's dick?' I repeated, before flicking my way through the hospital doctor's expert medical statement again.

'I'm sure that must be a new medical term for it Tommy. But I doubt very much, if it'll make it into the *British Medical Journal*!

What a Plonker!

...

All dressed up in our casual clothes for a shift night out, we decided to meet up at a local pub, within our working area.

As we all sat around, with numerous drinks in front of us and taking up several of the tables, the door opened and in came a typical Glesca punter, dressed in a black jerkin and black baseball cap, carrying a large, fully-laden sports bag.

He walked up to our table and bending down to open up his sports bag to display the contents, he pulled out some really nice colourful T-shirt tops and said, 'Right guys, if you're interested in a bargain, I'm prepared to let you have these, for a steal!'

Then jokingly he added, 'Mind you, if the polis stop you, I'll deny I sold them to you!'

He then paused for a moment and looked around at us all staring straight at him, then, shaking his head, he threw his arms out by his side and said, 'What?'

The reaction from us all was as one, as we produced our Police Warrant Identification Cards in unison, at our cocky little Del Boy Trotter.

As he focused on them, first, there was shock! Secondly, there was horror! And thirdly, there was a loud, 'Whoosh'! 'Bang'! 'Wallop'!

He was off like an Excocet missile, leaving the bar doors swinging in his wake along with some tasty designer T-shirts in his fully laden sports bag!

It wasn't long before he was apprehended, with the many volunteer witnesses present, all too keen to accept a recall to duty and the guaranteed overtime payment that goes with it!

To crown it all off, his real name was Roddy Bain, full name Rodney!

What a Plonker!

We Live in a Concrete Jungle

Tank, the likeable rogue, who was the scrap metal man, around the Bridgeton area of Glesca, where he lived, decided to take the wife and weans, away for a day, to the Blair Drummond Safari Park.

All packed up with the sandwiches and bottles of Irn Bru, they were off to spend a day with nature and wildlife!

After stopping at several interesting spots on their way around and enjoying the view of the various animals on show, they stopped to see if they could spot any lions!

'Oh look, Dad – there's a sign! We're in the Dangeroos area!' 'Let's see if we can spot Flipper hopping aboot mad!' Said one of the kids.

'That's no' "Dangeroos" son,' replied Tank, 'It's a sign saying, "Beware, *Dangerous* Area! Anyway, you'd have a hard job spotting Flipper, cause he was a dolphin, ya wee tottie!'

'Oh so he wiz! Ah meant to say Zippy!'

'Ye meant tae say Skippy!' said his Mum.

They sat in their van for quite a while, waiting patiently to hopefully catch a glimpse of a lion, but to no avail.

Getting slightly frustrated and restless, the kids, decided to open the side door of the van for some fresh air and slip outside to stretch their legs and maybe even have the obligatory pee against the side of the van.

No sooner had the kids got out, when all hell broke loose.

Loud sirens and wailing horns went off at a high pitch, terrifying the poor weans, who all panicked and promptly, jumped back into the van slamming the door shut.

Moments later, two Land Rovers with safari park rangers, all kitted out, came screeching to a halt, alongside their van.

As the rangers got out and pulled the side door open to check everything was all right with them, the weans, terrified by the alarms sounding and the appearance of the park rangers, blurted out in a true Glaswegian fashion, together as one, 'We never touched yer fucken lions!'

Cobblers

. . .

A prisoner was released after serving twenty-five years in prison.

As he searched through his property, he finds a receipt in his jacket pocket for a cobblers.

He made his way to the repair shop and handed the receipt over to the cobbler, who studied it carefully for a moment.

'Were they a pair of brown brogues, to be soled and healed?' He asked.

'Aye, that's right!' said the prisoner.

To which the cobbler responded, 'Be ready Friday!'

Roast Chicken and Chips

· · ·

I think all the resident nutcases in the areas where I worked, waited until I was on nightshift duty, so they could pay me a visit at the police station and obtain some free counselling sessions, followed by a cigarette, a cup of tea and a chocolate biscuit.

At one point, I was performing that many counselling sessions I thought I was employed by the NHS.

One of my many regular visitors was a larger-than-life woman called Georgina Hill, or Georgie, as she preferred to be called.

Georgie was a big woman in every sense of the word and I would describe her as a female, not blessed with the best of looks. Suffice to say, when she put her make up on she had a face like a Hallowe'en cake in Gregg's window display.

Obviously, mirrors were a novelty in her house.

She was also excessively overweight by several kilos and with her womanly body shape stuffed into a tweed coat that was several sizes too small for her, she resembled a burst sofa!

Now that I have dispensed with the pleasantries, I will relate my story to you.

The station door opened just after midnight and in breezed Georgie.

'Hello, Mr Morris. Just popped in to see how you are and have a wee blether with you!' she said.

'I'm fine thanks, Georgie. What about yourself? I haven't seen you around the Main Street for a few weeks?' I replied.

That was my first big mistake of the night! It was the cue for Georgie to begin relating her entire medical history, pausing only to catch a breath!

'Well, I don't think I told you but I've been in hospital. I was suffering from a bit of woman trouble!'

She then proceeded to perform a Les Dawson female impersonation, followed by a mime-artist impression as she pointed to her fat belly!

'All oot! All oot!' she said as she made hand signs across her stomach like she was signing into a meeting of the Masonic Lodge.

Her voice became quieter and as her actions became more animated, the more serious her operation sounded.

'Anyway!' she continued, 'the surgeon opened me up right across my stomach and done the business. I was that wide open they had to call in an upholsterer from, DFS to staple my wound together. The nurses said, "Georgie, what a mess you were in hen! That was major woman problems you had!" D'you know, Harry, see after that operation, I was bloody ravishing, I could've eaten a scabby cat 'atween two slice of stale bread . . .'

I interrupted her. 'I think you mean ravenous, Georgie!'

'Same thing, Harry!' she said dismissively. 'Anyway, the staff nurse said, "I'm sorry Georgie, but ye cannae eat, You'll need to wait for the doctor to come round first. Then they started all the small talk with me, like, "Have you got any kids Georgie?" and "Are they boys or lassies?"

'Well bugger me! Pardon my expression, but by this time, my stomach thinks that my throat's been cut during the operation and all they can talk aboot is kids! Now, don't get me wrong, Harry, I love kids and right at that moment I could probably have eaten a whole wan tae myself, but, right then all I'm thinking about, is Colonel Sanders' Kentucky Fried Chicken – I'll even pluck the thing myself!

'Anyways, next thing is, the nurse tells me they have a special surprise for me! "What is it?" I'm thinking to myself! Has the surgeon removed the wrong orgasms? Has he lost his Rolex watch? Or maybe they've found bits of Shergar inside me, 'cause that butcher in the main street is definitely dodgy – or maybe he just fancies me.

'Gonnae put me oot my bloody misery and tell me? I said to them.

'They both looked at each other for a moment, before the staff nurse said, "Right, after you've had a nice hot bath, I've arranged for the kitchen staff to make your favourite meal – roast chicken and chips, just for you!"

'Oh ya wee dancer!' I said. 'I hope it's legs are the size of an ostrich, 'cause I'm feeling pure anorexic!' Well, you never seen anybody get in and oot a bath as quick as me and when ah looked at my old Jean Brodie, with all they staples across it, I resembled a centre page, of wan o' my weans school jotters! It was the first time I had seen myself in a full-length mirror and my big jazz drum was sticking oot, like a pigeon's landing board! I kid you not you could've balanced a tray o' drinks on my erse! Anyway, I'm diverting again. However, I'm oot the bath and I'm drying myself and just as I lifted my left leg up tae dry my feet – guess whit?'

She then performed her Les Dawson impression again and started mouthing, 'Some o' the staples started popping and I thought I was gonnae burst oot all over the floor.' (God forbid! That's me thinking to myself!)

'Ah shouted for the nurses, but it was really another upholsterer I needed. The nurses came rushing in and whisked me away – I had to get emergency treatment and the next thing I know, they've put me on a drip and gave me an emergency blood transmission to replace what I had lost!

'As if that wasn't enough, the nurse then tells me, "I'm sorry Georgie, but you can't have anything to eat!"

'I said, Whit! Are you yanking my chain? I've had that Nil by Mouth sign up on my bed that long, my family thinks that's my real name in French!

Just at that the auxiliary nurse comes over to me and asks, "Do you need a bed pan, Georgie?"

'Ah said, are you trying to take the piss? You need to eat, before you can excrete!' I then turned my attention back to the nurse and said, 'And who is going to get my roast chicken and chips then?'

"The bin!" she replied. "The cook threw it out." Now, as she put her arm across me to tidy my bed sheet, I thought about biting it aff!'

Just at that point, there was a noise at the rear of the police station and the door was opened and I could hear my police colleagues coming in for their tea break.

Interrupting Georgie in full flow, I said, 'Well Georgie, I could sit and listen to you going through your entire medical history, but I'll need to interrupt you, because that's the boys in the police panda arriving for their refreshment period and you'll never guess what I'm going to have for my dinner?'

She stared at me for a moment, before a smile broke out across her face and she said in an excited voice, 'Roast chicken and chips!'

To which I replied, 'No hen, three quarters of an hour like everybody else!'

Good night, Georgie!

J.F.K.

. . .

Many police officers of a certain age remember where they were on that fateful day when President John F. Kennedy was assassinated.

Although such an event sticks in the memories of our older colleagues, it is sometimes a surprise to learn, that more than half the world has only just been born since then.

With this in mind, two police officers in the city centre were interviewing a not-to-bright female suspect.

When asked for her date of birth, she replied, 'The twenty-second of November 1963!'

The older cop, immediately recognising the significance of the date said, 'I bet your mother remembers where she was when John F. Kennedy was shot dead?'

At which point the female suspect immediately protested in a rant, 'My mammy knows 'nuthin' about any shooting! She's no' intae that kind o' stuff! Who says she is? I'm her daughter and I have a right to know exactly what she's accused of and who grassed her up!'

Needless to say, both cops just looked at each other slightly bemused and shook their heads.

Dr White at Your Disposal

• • •

Whilst on duty one night in the station, I was sorting through some reports when the front door burst open and in came a known offender in his mid-twenties, who ran past me into a back room.

The male was known to me as the son of a convicted drug dealer in the area, who had taken over the family business.

As I went through to the back office after him, he was holding his chin together, with blood streaming profusely, from a large deep laceration. It's usually caused by someone slashing you with a Stanley knife or similar and is often referred to as a Kirk Douglas!

He was scared and screaming frantically, 'Help me! I'm getting chased wi' a team and they're tooled up wi' blades!'

Suddenly, I heard a loud disturbance outside and I saw about eight youths, staring over at me from the pedestrian walkway, armed with knives and clubs.

I immediately lifted the office radio and called for assistance, whereby on seeing this, the youths all ran off.

My next priority was to try and stem the flow of blood from his serious facial injury and summon the assistance of an ambulance.

Using paper towels and applying pressure to the wound, I was able to stem the flow of blood, while I searched through the office first-aid kit for a bandage. However the items inside were so old, they would not be out of place on the *Antique Roadshow*! The sterile pads would've given him gangrene!

At this point I noticed on the wall of the female officers' toilet, a Dr White sanitary towel machine.

Now they're most definitely sterile!

Out of sight of my young gangster victim, I quickly ripped open the small package and removed the sanitary towel, which was a pad about four inches in length, with a hoop at either end.

Removing the sodden bloodstained paper towels from his face, I replaced them with the sanitary towel, covering the wound, and unable to resist it, I looped the hoops on either end, over his ears, to hold it in place.

(Why hoops I'll never know? But I'll accept explanations on a stamped address envelope. From women only!)

I then told him to apply pressure to it.

He sat quietly, for the first time the victim of a crime, while awaiting the arrival of the ambulance, totally unaware of what the sterile dressing on his chin was.

That was, however, until four of my police colleagues arrived at the office, in response to my call for assistance.

As they rushed in, they instantly recognised the victim, who was sitting quietly feeling sorry for himself, with his hammock-style dressing dangling from his ears. This was the cue for them to start asking, 'So Harry, are you taking first period for your break, or second period?'

They just could not contain themselves as they fell about laughing and making trivial excuses to the victim, in order to leave the office.

A few minutes later, the ambulance arrived and after a few titters of laughter from the paramedic crew, they soon removed the injured man, complete with sanitary towel stuck to his chin, to the local accident and emergency hospital.

After they had left, as you would imagine, there was the usual lengthy 'period' of sick jokes from the cops who were present.

Particularly, as this was the beginning of the festive 'period'!

Prison Riot Solution

...

My brother Freddie related a story that he heard, during a golf club function.

The guest speaker was a former deputy prison warden and he was explaining that, while employed by the prison service, he was performing duties as acting governor of the prison, when staff contacted him at home regarding a riot taking place within the prison.

They also informed him that several of the inmates had climbed on to the roof and were ripping the slates off and hurling them into the prisoners' exercise yard.

He immediately attended at the prison to assess the situation and was quickly briefed on his arrival by his senior officer, on duty.

He then went out into the yard, where a few of the trustee prisoners, were attempting to clear up the debris.

With the aid of a loudspeaker, he tried to reason with the rebellious inmates, protesting on the rooftop of the jail, but to no avail, as the prisoners ignored his request to come down and discus matters.

As he stood there, frantically wracking his brain for an amicable solution to this problem, he overheard one of the trustees in the yard, mention that he knew how to get them down off the roof.

'Why didn't I think of that?' he thought to himself. 'If anybody knows how to get a con off the roof, it's another con himself!'

Convinced of this, he nonchalantly sidled over to the trustee and said, 'Tell me something Coutts – if you were in my position, how would you get those prisoners off the roof?'

To which Coutts confidently replied in all seriousness, 'Very easily Guvnor! I'd shoot the bastards!'

Open the Door

• • •

Late one night, I received a call that a certain person wanted on warrant by the police, was within a house in the Rutherglen area.

Accompanied by three other cops, I attended at the address given and so as not to spook our wanted person, I parked the police van several metres away, out of sight and we walked to the building to avoid being seen.

The entrance to the tenement had a security controlled system, with buzzers for each flat.

In order not to warn our wanted person, I buzzed the ground floor apartment, which had a light on.

'Who is it?' screeched a woman's voice over the intercom.

'It's the police ma'am!' I replied quietly. 'Can you let me into the building please?'

'Who did you say you were?' she asked.

'It's the police ma'am!' I repeated in a soft voice.

'What are you whispering for then?' she said.

'Because, we need to gain entry quietly!' I replied.

'Why?! What's up?' she asked.

'Nothing to alarm you ma'am, I just require to gain entry to the building.' I repeated.

'Don't you have a key then?' she asked me.

'No, ma'am, I don't have a key. Now can you please let me in the building?' I pleaded, trying to keep reasonably quiet and calm.

'Well, how do I know you're the polis?' she enquired.

I assured her, that I was and she need only to look out her window and she would see for herself.

This she did, by pulling her curtain to one side, where-upon she was able to view my three police colleagues and me, standing on the footpath, in full view, waving to her.

She then returned to her intercom and I stood at the door, ready to open it, when she buzzed.

'You don't look like polis,' she blurted out. 'Where's yer hats?'

I was becoming exasperated with her, but remained very calm.

'They're in the police van!' I replied. 'Now will you please open the door to the building and allow us access?'

She paused for a moment, then said, 'Whit polis van are ye referring tae, 'cause I don't see one?'

'That's because I parked it further along the road!' I said, trying not to lose my cool. 'Now will you buzz the door and let us in, please?' I repeated for the umpteenth time.

'Why did you park it further along the road?' she asked.

I then explained to her, we didn't want the person we were after, looking out his window and seeing us arrive in it. Although, by this time, I think most of the street knew of our presence.

Finally, she decided, she would let us in, but there was a delay.

'Now what's up?' I asked her.

'It's my buzzer – it's stuck!' she said.

'That doesn't surprise me, missus. You probably don't use it enough!' I replied facetiously.

It was then decided, she would come out to the front of the building and unlock the door, but she would only do it, if we stood far enough back from the door entrance.

Reluctantly, I agreed to her request and we all stood back as she tiptoed to the outside door and pulling it open, she ran back to her house.

Guess what? As I approached the door – bang!- it closed shut. I got back onto the intercom and informed her, we did not gain entry, as the door had closed before we could reach it. So would she mind opening it again!

Like before, we had to stand well back from the entrance.

We were all becoming so frustrated with her, so much so, we were seriously considering rushing the door as she opened it this time.

I also suggested we forget about our wanted person and just arrest her instead! Jokingly, of course!!

Eventually, we gained entry to the building and guess what? There was no trace of our suspect!

I just wonder how he knew we were coming!

Soft Hands That Do Dishes

· · ·

The makers of Fairy Liquid are making a new advert for their washing-up liquid and it's to be filmed in the Gorbals, Glasgow.

Here's a sneak preview of the script, written in typical Glesca dialogue.

'Hey Maw, how's yer hauns sae saft?'

To which the mother replies, 'Cause I'm only fucken thirteen ya eejit!'

It's Good Too Talk

. . .

A newly promoted superintendent arrived at his appointed sub-divisional office, to take up his new tenure.

Like all promoted officers, on the first day at a new station, he was eager to make a quick impression with the office staff.

As he sat down at his desk, he took time to survey all around him.

Suddenly, there was a knock at his office door. He quickly picked up the telephone on his desk and put it to his ear, whereby he then called out, 'Come in!'

The door opened and in walked the elderly duty desk sergeant.

The superintendent placed his hand over the mouthpiece and said, 'Be with you in a minute, sergeant. Just wait there!'

The following, is the one-sided conversation that took place.

'Yes John, [the name of a former chief constable] I'm settling in fine, thank you! What about you? How is retirement? Good, I'm glad to hear it, because, I know from talking to Willie [the new chief constable] you're going to be a very hard act to follow!'

The elderly desk sergeant stood patiently waiting, looking around the room uneasily and tapping his foot on the floor!

'Anyway, John, I'll have to go now. I've someone desperately waiting to see me – you know what it is like at the top – so I'll speak to you later!'

At that point he replaced the telephone handset and looked up at the elderly sergeant, who was still patiently waiting.

'Right sergeant, what can I do for you then?' he asked.

To which the elderly sergeant replied, 'It was just to let you know, sir, that the engineer from British Telecom is here to re-connect your telephone . . . When you're finished using it!'

The Taxi
. . .

One morning a policewoman colleague overslept for her early shift duty.

Quick as a flash, she jumped out of bed and whilst pulling on her uniform, she called for a taxi.

Several minutes later she made her way downstairs and was standing just outside the front door to her house, awaiting it's arrival, when a Vauxhall Cavalier motor car, was driven into the street, stopping outside her apartment block.

Closing her front door, she ran over to the car, opened the rear passenger door and got in.

Once inside, she noticed old newspapers, empty Coke cans and chocolate and sweet papers strewn about the back seat and floor.

Annoyed about the untidy state of the car, she said, in a rather indignant voice, to the driver, who by this time had turned around to look at his passenger, 'I think it is about time you had a valet done and washed out the back of this taxi, it's absolutely filthy!'

At which point the rather bemused elderly driver said, 'I'm sorry to disappoint you hen, but this isn't a taxi, I'm only here to collect my son for work!'

Exit a rather embarrassed policewoman!

What Do You Mean?

• • •

Whilst spending a few days seconded to the traffic speed radar squad, I was asked if I had brought a sandwich with me for my lunch or did I need to buy something from the local city baker's.

As it was, I had nothing with me so I opted to go to the baker's with Eddie Weldon and John Campbell, two members of the squad.

We all entered the shop together.

'Yes m'dear, what would you like?' enquired the stoutly built female shop assistant.

'I'll have a hot pie please.' I said.

The female assistant opened the hotplate cabinet and, picking up a pie, she placed it neatly onto a white paper napkin, before returning to the counter, where she asked, 'Would you like a wee poke with that?'

To which I immediately responded with, 'Not just now, hen, can you no' see I'm still working?'

Eddie and John almost choked at the thought and spent the rest of the entire day, relating the story to everybody we met!

Nurses Can't Be Trusted!

• • •

I had occasion to visit my partner Eddie O'Reilly in the Southern General Hospital, where he was admitted and placed in traction after a serious road accident on his police motorbike.

Whilst on duty, I was allowed to call in and see him, outwith normal visiting times available to members of the public.

On this particular day it was not long after the patients in the ward had been served their lunch and they were all settling down for a quiet period and the usual afternoon nap.

While sitting alongside his bed talking, O'Reilly interrupted me and said, 'Is the man in the next bed sleeping?'

I leaned forward on my seat to look at him.

'Aye, he's sound asleep.' I replied, unaware of what was coming next.

'Right!' said O'Reilly, 'reach over to his bed locker and grab a handful of his paper tissues!'

'Whit?' I said, surprised, while sitting there, decked out in my black leather police motorcycle uniform. 'No way! He might just waken up while I'm doing it and catch me in the act!'

'He won't waken up – they give him strong medication to make him sleep.' replied O'Reilly reassuringly! 'Now, stop being a drama queen, Harry and get them for me!'

'Let me get this right – you want me to steal some paper tissues from an unconscious patient on strong medication?' I asked him!

'I've told you, it's no' stealing, you're only borrowing them for me, 'cause I don't want to waken him up and ask him!' O'Reilly replied convincingly.

'Well okay,' I said reluctantly. 'But if he *does* waken up, you can do the explaining!'

I then leaned over, making certain he was asleep, before grabbing hold of several paper tissues, which I handed over to O'Reilly.

I was somewhat puzzled as to why he wanted them, but oh boy, was I in for a shock? Taking hold of the tissues in one hand, he then reached up with his other hand and grabbed hold of the metal traction framework above his head. He then pulled himself up from his hospital bed and with the hand clutching the paper tissues, he put them behind his back. Whereby, to my utter disbelief, he wiped his bare backside with them!

He then produced the brown soiled tissues for me to view and said, in total disgust, 'I knew it! That bloody young nurse, isn't wiping my arse properly!'

He then tried to hand the soiled tissues to me to dispose of, but, by this time, I had buggered off down the stairs, mounted my motorcycle and was half way along the Govan Road before you could say Andrex.

However, having borrowed the paper tissues, like he said he was doing, I often wondered if he ever put them back.

'YUCK!'

Watch Yer Car Mister?

. . .

On football match days in Glasgow, it was the normal for motorists parking their cars near to the stadium, to be surrounded with a posse of young boys who immediately offered their services to the drivers, 'Watch yer motor for you, mister? It doesn't cost much.'

Each and every individual car owner would be offered their safeguard services.

The practice was, to agree to their request and give them some loose change from your pocket and promise them more on your return. This would make sure your car was safe, for the entire duration of the football match.

On this particular match day, a new Vauxhall Frontera jeep drove up and out got two well-dressed male occupants.

As usual, the posse descended on them, offering their services to the driver.

'Watch yer motor for you mister?' they asked.

'No thanks, boys. No need for you – Rolex will watch it for me!' the driver replied smugly, pointing to a large Alsatian dog, sitting in the rear of the jeep, which began barking ferociously and baring its teeth at the young boys present. 'He's a watchdog!'

Both males then walked off hooting with laughter.

Two hours later, you can picture the look of horror on their faces when they returned to find their Frontera jeep, sitting up on concrete bricks with Rolex still inside, but minus four expensive alloy wheels.

Under the front windscreen wiper, there was a note which read,

Ye're right, mister, it is a watchdug. It watched us while we blagged yer wheels, ya big diddy!'

Who Are You – Pinnochio?
. . .

One Monday morning, while working dock duty at the High Court, in Glasgow. I was having a cup of tea, when I looked up and saw this pretty young policewoman, coming towards me.

'Hi Uncle Harry, I bet you're surprised to see me?' she said.

It was the daughter of one of my closest friends. 'What are you doing here?' I asked her.

'I've been assigned here for the entire week!' she replied.

She sat down and I introduced her to the other cops present – some of them knew of her dad.

After exchanging some updated gossip with her, I went to see the duty officer and arranged for her to work with me for the rest of the week, as she was a nice, quiet, reserved girl.

I then phoned her dad at his CID office and told him I was working with her and I would make sure, she would be all right.

Later the same day, we had just come down from the court for lunch and as usual, had to pass a cell full of accused prisoners due up in the court that day.

As we were passing, one of them shouted out, 'Hey sweetheart, gonnae sit on my face?'

Quick as a flash, she responded with, 'Why? Is your nose bigger than your penis?'

The other prisoners burst out laughing at this impromptu reply and, as we walked on, he was being pelted with verbal abuse from his other cellmates!

Needless to say, I phoned her dad and told him that I thought she'd be okay!

The Pink Slip

• • •

A regular occurrence on a Wednesday morning at the police station was being inundated by members of the public claiming to have lost the cash from their state benefit Giro cheque – on their way back from the post office to the shops!

They never, ever lost their Giro cheque – it was always their money, immediately after they had cashed their Giro cheque.

The common practice was, should this unfortunate incident occur, to call at the local police office and make a loss report to the police, then obtain a 'pink slip' receipt confirming you had reported the loss. Thereafter, you would attend, with your pink slip at the local DHSS office and receive a crisis loan, for the amount of cash you allegedly lost.

Whether anyone ever repaid the crisis loan is another story!

Due to this continual practice, the cops and station assistants were becoming more frustrated and infuriated, in particular with the same old faces presenting the same set of circumstances, every other week, as to how they had inadvertently lost their Giro money.

One alleged loser, came up with a novel excuse, which just has to be shared.

Having called at the police station, under the influence of alcohol, he reported he had lost his Giro cheque cash.

When I asked him where he had lost it, he supplied me with the following account, in a slurred and drunken Glaswegian voice.

'Right big man, I'm gonnae tell ye the whole truth, right!' (Well that's a good start!)

'This is absolutely genuine big man. Ye're never gonnae believe it. Just wait tae ah tell ye this! See, I've cashed my Giro, right? And I had a right dose o' fucken' toothache. Oops! Sorry for swearing, big man – just a wee slip-up! Know whit a mean? Anyway, ah had a right dose o' the effen toothache!'

He then put his hand into his mouth. Pulling it open and pointing with his other hand, he said, 'That bastert right there! Well, it's no' there noo, 'cause it's oot, but I'm telling ye exactly whit happened, big man, as God is my – hic! – judge! Right, so ah said to mysel', "Dentist, my man!"' He paused for a moment to think, then repeated, 'Dentist?'

He screwed his eyes up and scratched his head while talking to himself. Then he snapped his fingers!

'Ah mean, "Dennis, my man." Forgot ma fucken name there for a minute! Oh, sorry, man, jist slipped oot again! Sorry!

'Anyway, Ah said tae mysel', "Dennis, you need to go and see the dennist! So ah made my way up tae the Dental Hospital, right? And yer man, the dennist says tae me, "Dennis! Ye're needin' a few o' yer munchers out, son, so, I'm gonnae gie ye a wee dose o' gas, OK?" Noo, Who am I tae argue wi' the dennist, he knows the score and he's a big b-ba-ba––'

I interrupted him before he repeated it. 'Dennis!'

He continued, 'ba-balack guy, so Ah said tae him, "You're the boss big man. Fill yer boots, but jist don't shrink my heid! Right?" Well! when I've woke up, my gub was full o' blood and I was feeling like I'd just smoked some right heavy Moroccan wacky backy, 'cause ma heid's pure dizzy, right? And this is whit Ah think happened.

'Noo, listen up! Ah think, I've taken my Giro money oot and when I went tae put it back into my poacket Ah've missed and it's dropped oot, oan tae the grun' below! Noo! Whit dae ye think yersel', big yin? Does that no' sound like a pure genuine story?'

He then threw his hands out by his side and said, in a Tommy Cooper voice and visual impersonation, 'The whole truth big man, just like' – hic! – that!'

I stood there staring at him for a moment, in total amazement, trying to digest this remarkable tale of woe, in fact, it cheered me up, being one of the best I've ever heard.

All the while he stood there in front of me, demonstrating with his hands how he could have missed his pocket. And then, pulling at his mouth, opening it wide, to expose this black crater where he once had teeth.

After giving his scenario some serious thought for a few moments, I said, 'So, you're saying you lost your Giro money, when you were at the dentist having some teeth removed. Is that right?'

He snapped his fingers then, offered up his hand to shake mine, he said, 'Ye're absolutely spot on, big man. That's exactly whit I've been tellin' ye.' Hic! Now ye're talking!'

'Well,' I said, 'might I suggest you rush home to your house and check under your pillow and see if the Tooth Fairy has been and left you any cash! . . . Because you're not getting a pink slip from me. Now get lost!'

Who Let Them Go?

· · ·

One day at the police headquarters, I had arranged a visitation for a local Boys' Brigade' outfit and while escorting them around the office and taking them into the various rooms, for example, fingerprinting, taped interview room and the cells, etc. Some of the boys had wandered off by themselves into a room displaying several male photographs on one part of the wall, with a sign above, which read, 'Top Ten List'.

'Who are they?' asked one small boy.

Exaggerating my answer, to make their visit more interesting for them, I said, 'Those are photographs of the ten most wanted men in Scotland!'

The same small boy, pointing to the wall, enquired again. 'They're the ten most wanted men in Scotland?'

'That's correct.' I replied forthrightly.

'Well,' said the young boy, pausing for a moment. 'Don't you think it would have been a good idea to lock them up in prison when you were taking their photographs?'

Don't you just love kids?

Sumjerk Ramdmakhar

. . .

Being able to impersonate various accents comes in handy, particularly when the cops in the office, from time to time, would ask me to make calls for them, in order to wind up someone in another office or department.

This was the case on one day, with a male civilian assistant, when the cops working out of his office were fed up with the way he spoke to members of the public and wanted me to set him up.

I decided I would call him and report a hit and run road accident, in a Pakistani/Indian accent.

The telephone was answered by my victim. 'Strathclyde Police Pollokshaws. Can I help you?'

'Hello, sir, I am vanting to report a car has just collided with my car and the driver is trying to drive off!' I said.

'Where are you sir?' he asked.

'I'm here in the telephone box calling you!' I replied.

'Yes, I know that sir, but where?' he repeated.

'Where the telephone box has always been – in the same street vhere my car has been hit!' I replied sarcastically.

'Right, well let me put it to you this way, where has your car been hit, then?' he asked.

'On the side of it – big bash, dreadful damage to my car. My vife, she's very upset by this big bugger!' I answered back.

Becoming slightly frustrated by my evasive answers, he said, 'Sir, as much as I appreciate what you are saying, I need to know the name of the street where the accident has taken place.'

'Vell vhy didn't you just ask me that first?' I rudely replied.

'I did sir, but you obviously misunderstood me.' he said.

'I'm not remembering you asking me that. Maybe you are talking too fast for me to be understanding you!' I responded.

By this time I could hear him breathing heavily and could picture his face, with steam coming out of his ears.

'OK, sir! Can...you...tell...me...your...name...please?' he asked me in a deliberately slow and sarcastic manner.

'My...name...is...Sumjerk...Ramdmakhar! Do...you...understand...me?' I replied facetiously.

'There's no need for that attitude sir!' he said.

'Vell, you started it!' I answered back.

'OK, let's not argue about it ...Mr Sum...jerk Ramd...ma...khar! Is that how you pronounce your name?'

At this point the penny dropped and I could hear him repeating my name to himself, under his breath, 'Sum...jerk Ramd...ma...khar! Some Jerk Rammed My Car!'

'Right you bastard, who is this? I'm on to you!'

'I'm begging your pardon sir, but vhy do you call me bastard?' I asked him.

'You know exactly why, you bastard. Anyway, I know who you are!' he said, annoyed by the wind-up, but more so that he'd been duped.

However, if you buy the book, you will know who Sum...Jerk was!

And it wasn't me!

The Mushroom Joke

· · ·

Alan White was a detective sergeant I worked with who was too polite to be a cop. Here is a typical situation I had with him one day.

During a tea-break in the office, I was sitting telling him a joke, which went like this. 'Did you hear about the wee mushroom who went out drinking and dancing every night?' I then paused for a moment before continuing. 'He was a "fun-gi" to be with!'

Alan laughed and said, 'That was a good one, Harry. I must remember it!'

Later the same day, I entered the office and Alan was with the detective inspector and a few other CID officers.

'Wait till I tell you this joke!' he said very enthusiastically. With the complete attention of all who were present, he said, 'What do you call a wee mushroom who goes out dancing and drinking every night with all his friends?'

'I don't know.' Said one of the officers.

Whereby Alan replied, 'A "fun-fellow" to be with!'

I swear he got a bigger laugh than I did and I told the joke right!

A Tight Situation

• • •

Along with another motorcycle colleague, we were patrolling the Springburn area of Glasgow, when we were signalled to stop by a concerned female home-help.

She had called at one of her elderly lady clients and was unable to gain entry to her house.

However, the elderly lady's Labrador dog, could be heard whining and yelping inside, an indication that the lady was possibly there, but none of the neighbours had seen or heard from her.

I attended along with the home-help to the house, situated within a tenement building, but I was unable to see inside her windows, due to the curtains being drawn shut.

Meanwhile, my colleague made enquiries as to who might have seen her last and how long the dog had been yelping, but nobody could shed any light on our enquiries with regards to her most recent sighting.

I had to accept the fact that she may have suffered a sudden illness or, injury and had collapsed in an unconscious state.

The first obstacle I encountered was the letterbox which I had to try and clear of the stuffed newspapers that were blocking it.

Having achieved this, I was met with the wet, heavy panting of her excited dog, which was obviously desperate to get out.

All the while I was positive I could hear a weird moaning sound coming from inside, but it certainly was not coming from the dog.

I decided to refrain from wasting any more precious time and with no other option available, I decided to force entry, as I feared she might be lying severely injured.

After several attempts, using bodily force and kicking the door, it finally succumbed to my size nine Doc Marten boot pressure.

These Docs were responsible for demolishing many a door.

The poor desperate dog, forced its way past everybody out onto the landing to get to the back door and out to the garden for a much needed and overdue pee.

My colleague, Ian Thomson, along with the home-help, both feared the worst for the elderly woman and prompted me to enter the house first and check for her.

As I made my way along the small entrance hallway, checking each room in turn, I arrived at the kitchen.

Looking inside, I couldn't stop myself from smiling.

'Are you OK hen?' I asked the frail figure, lying on the kitchen floor staring back at me.

'I think so, but I've lost all feeling in my legs. I think I might be paralysed. I can't move them!' she replied.

At this point I summoned the assistance of the home-help.

After a short chat, a hot cup of tea and a massage to get the circulation flowing in her legs again, she was able to tell me, that after her supper, the night before, she was sitting on a small stool in the kitchen, pulling on her warm thermal tights, when she somehow managed to squeeze both feet into the same leg of her tights.

She then pulled them on so tightly that she couldn't move.

Due to this action and being unable to move, she then lost her balance and fell over onto the kitchen floor.

Thinking that she was somehow paralysed, she lay motionless on the kitchen floor all night.

No doubt, the first job for the home-help that morning, was to go out and buy her a pair of thermal socks!

You're Nicked!

. . .

Having received numerous weekly complaints from a local MP about the amount of car drivers exceeding the speed limit, along the roadway, past his house, my partner and I were sent to the location, in order to use the new Muni-Quip speed gun.

Now the speed gun is a hand-held device. You point it in the direction of oncoming traffic and it registers, on a small screen, the speed of the vehicle.

After several minutes of setting up and checking our equipment, we were set to begin operating.

Moments later our first car arrived and it was being driven at excessive speed. I pointed the speed gun at it and – Bingo! It registered 44 mph. My partner signalled the oncoming driver to pull over and stop.

The driver was made aware of why he had been stopped and shown his registered speed on the screen, after which he said, 'But you can't charge me! I'm the local MP for the area who wrote in and complained about the amount of drivers speeding!'

'Well sir!' I replied, 'you'll be able tell your constituents and write in and inform my supervisor that you saw at first hand, the police officers in attendance, performing their duty and catching the offenders responsible!'

Answer The Phone!

· · ·

Along with my colleague, I called at the home of David Dick in order to execute a Sheriff's apprehension warrant.

Having knocked on his door several times and received no response, I was about to leave, when I noticed the house keys were in the inside door lock.

This prompted me to look through the letterbox and on doing so I noticed a telephone on a table in the entrance hallway.

I left and went down to the lower landing of the tenement building out of earshot and contacted my police radio controller at the station and asked him to look the local telephone book for David Dick's home telephone number.

Bingo! His number was listed, so I now requested the radio controller to call him.

I then went back upstairs to his door, lifted the letterbox and waited.

Moments later, the telephone began to ring in the hallway. It rang several times then, unable to resist a telephone ringing, David Dick appeared in the hallway from a nearby room.

I watched him through the letterbox opening, as he slowly and deliberately, tip-toed in typical *Pink Panther* cartoon fashion, towards the telephone and picking it up, he put it to his ear, then answered it in a soft whispering voice, 'Hello!'

To which the police radio controller on the other end of the telephone responded by saying, 'Hello, is that David Dick?'

'Yes.' Dick replied in a whisper.

The controller then said, 'Well, it's the police here, would you kindly go over and open the door to the officers waiting outside, who wish to serve you with an apprehension warrant for your arrest?!'

Dick slowly turned around to see me peering at him through the letterbox, but having seen the funny side of it all, he burst out laughing and eventually opened the door to us.

That's What She Said!
• • •

Whilst checking a statement taken by a young recruit, regarding a road accident, I came across the following given by the female driver, 'As a result of the accident, I have a large bruise on my buttocks, bruises to my back and my face is sore. I'm also nine months pregnant'!

CSI Not Required
• • •

I attended the scene of a housebreaking and while looking at the point of entry, it was obvious to me the person responsible used a true or false key to get in.

I immediately suspected an inside job by the householder, or that one of her sons present, was involved.

I was about to put my theory into practice with the lady of the house, when I noticed a piece of paper with writing on it, which she had left, pinned on the back door of her house for her sons. It read, 'Gone out to the shops, won't be long, love mum. PS, the keys are in the usual place. In the yellow peg bag hanging on the washing line!'

Dusty Bin

• • •

As I walked into the motorcycle cops' canteen kitchen, Adam Cook was in the process of making himself a pot of tea, with his lunch box lying open on the worktop, containing two sandwiches an apple and a chocolate biscuit.

A shout rang out from another part of the office, 'Adam Cook, you're wanted on the telephone!'

I looked at him and said, 'Go get the telephone Adam and I'll make your tea for you"

'Thanks Harry!' He said, handing me the teapot.

While standing there making the tea for Adam, the door opened and in walked Dusty Bin, aptly named, because, he was one greedy fat bastard who ate non-stop.

He walked over and looked into Adam's lunch box and said, 'Whit have ye got for yer lunch then Harry?' Poking at the sandwiches with his fingers.

'Nothing much!' I replied, giving him the impression it was my lunchbox. 'I had fish and chips earlier at the training school, so I'm pretty much full up!'

'Are you going to eat these sandwiches then?' he enquired.

'Definitely not!' I replied. 'I couldn't possibly eat anything else, it would just be greed and totally out of order.'

'Do you mind if I help myself?' he asked pleadingly.

'Do what you want, Dusty. I'm certainly not going to eat them!' I replied.

'Oh thanks Harry, you're a gentleman,' he replied, promptly helping himself to one of the sandwiches from the lunch box.

As he munched away on it, he said, 'Mmmm! They're tasty Harry, tell your missus she makes a mean sandwich!'

'I'll tell her, but my missus never made them.' I responded.

'Well, whoever made them, they're bloody good!' he replied.

I then remarked as I walked out of the kitchen, 'Yeah, they certainly look good – wire in!'

'Can I have the other one?' He called out, as I entered the rest room, carrying Adam's pot of tea.

'Do what you like, I'm not going to eat them, that's for sure!' I replied, as I sat down in the rest room, directly opposite the canteen entrance, closely followed by Dusty, armed with an apple in one hand and a half eaten second sandwich in the other.

'There's no way you made these yersel' Harry, so tell yer wife, she makes a damn good sandwich!' he reiterated.

'What, them?' I said, 'No way, my missus made them. Unless she's having an affair that I don't know about!'

A few minutes later, the door opened and Adam entered the rest room and looking at us both, he said, 'Right! Where's my sandwiches? Where did you hide them?'

I immediately said, 'Well, tell him Dusty! You were in the kitchen last!'

Dusty Bin gulped in horror, realising what I had done to him, before performing an excellent impersonation of an Ardrossan Seagull, as he tried to swallow his stolen Adam's apple whole!

Playing It Cool

...

In the late seventies, I was on mobile patrol with Tam Spencer and Jim McGhee. We were patrolling the Queenspark area of Glasgow, where a pro IRA demonstration march had been taking place.

During his days off, Tam, worked as a coal man, doing deliveries, carrying the heavy laden sacks filled with coal, up and down tenement stairs. He was about 5' 10" in height with hands like shovels and the thickest neck I have ever seen, being as broad as his shoulders and I kid you not.

The expression, built like a 'brick shit-house' readily comes to mind when I think of Tam.

Anyways, during our patrol we received a call to attend the Royal Marines Territorial Army Halls in Maxwell Road regarding a complaint of a part-time marine having been seriously assaulted by a mob that had just entered a nearby public house.

Having attended and taken the necessary particulars required for a crime report, one young soldier described the main instigator involved as a male in his early thirties, short black dyed hair with a bright red V neck jumper.

Tam being the senior cop said, 'Right guys, here's how we play it. We're going into the lion's den here, because this place is bursting at the seams with demonstrators and sympathisers, so let's play it cool.

'Firstly, when we go in, keep your back to the door and slide in along the wall, without causing too much fuss. Once inside, we survey the crowd and see if we can identify our man. If we see him, I'll quietly and peacefully, saunter over to him and invite him to come outside to talk, but whatever you do, do not take your baton out, okay? You must not show any sign of aggression.'

Having been briefed by Tam as to how we were going to deal with the situation, the three of us entered the pub, where inside the atmosphere and mood of the place could only be described as ugly.

Fortunately, we spotted our suspect immediately, sitting at a table to our right, near the door with about nine or ten other males.

The table was full of pints of beer with a large cigarette ashtray about 10" in diameter on the center of the table.

Tam leaned across the table and asked the suspect politely, if he could speak with him outside.

'Are you blind big man? Can ye no' see I'm drinking and I've just got a round in for the table?' Replied the male suspect, as his friends sitting alongside him laughed at his response. He then lifted up a pint glass of beer and drank it down, after which, he then put the glass back on the table and joined in the laughter with his friends.

Big mistake! Not a man to mess with, Tam remained very calm and again politely asked the suspect male to come outside so he could speak with him.

Having gained some bravado from his daily intake of alcohol, coupled with the support of his many friends sitting around the table with him, the suspect replied, 'Are you still here? Either get a round in or get yersel' tae fuck oot ma face, I'm busy!'

As he turned away, he picked up another pint glass of beer from the table and muttered under his breath, 'Arsehole!'

An even bigger mistake than the first as Tam leaned over the table and wrapped his hand around the ned's wee hand that was holding the pint glass and began to squeeze it. The ned squirmed with the pain and the thought that the glass would smash in his hand, he put it back on the table.

At this, Tam grabbed hold of his collar and with his other hand he picked up the large table ashtray and promptly walloped the ned across the head with it, whereby all hell broke out as Tam then hauled the ned over the table with glasses of beer spilling everywhere and smashing onto the floor.

Tam then dragged him past Jim and I, ushering him straight out the door, followed by us, but not before we stopped several objects with our bodies, such as bottles, glasses, ashtrays and other missiles, thrown in our direction.

Once outside, we were able to draw our batons and put them through the door handles to retain the irate punters inside just long enough for more police support to arrive and quell the situation.

As for our gallus suspect, by the time we arrived at the police office, he had turned into a sober, quiet little mouse of a man, with a thumping large lump on his head!

As for Tam, whenever I had the good fortune to work with him, I ignored all police strategy being spouted by him and just played it by ear. It was definitely a much safer option!

High Court Trial

. . .

During a trial at the High Court in Glasgow, a male witness was giving evidence and referred to himself as being a 'flying saucer', which he then explained to the assembled jury and the beleaguered judge, that it was a Glasgow term for a dosser or, down-and-out person, with a serious alcohol problem!

'You mean, you're an alcoholic, don't you?' asked the advocate depute (prosecution).

'Well, you could say that!' he replied.

'I *am* saying that, Mr Barnes!' said the depute. 'Now, tell me, when was the last time you worked?'

'The last time I worked, was the last time I was sober, sir!' he answered.

'And when was that?' asked the depute.

'I don't really remember, but it was a while ago!' he replied.

'OK!' said the depute, before changing direction. 'Tell me what you did on the day of the incident?'

'I bought a carry-oot wi' my Giro money and went to the bench in the park to drink it.' he said.

'And how long did you drink for?' enquired the depute.

The witness searched his brain for an answer, all the while pulling several funny facial expressions as he tried desperately to recall the moment. Then, his eyebrows raised and he proudly blurted out in all sincerity, 'Until I fell off the park bench pished, sir!'

A short adjournment had to be called, when the jury members, fell off their bench seats laughing!

Television Psychic

• • •

This is a story related to me by a TV licence detector van inspector.

While working in a certain area they had been detected by the locals who quickly spread the word of their presence around the housing scheme.

One particular female, who did not possess a valid TV licence, rushed up to her local post office straight away and purchased one.

As it was, the TV detector van, just happened to call into the street where she lived. The female, having obtained her licence, was heading out to her work and, on seeing the TV van she knocked on the window and said, 'If you're going to number six, tell my man, the TV licence is behind the big clock on the mantelpiece!'

With that said, she hurried on her way.

The TV licence inspector decided, since they were there, they might as well check it. They knocked on the door of number six and the husband, who was unaware of what had passed previously, answered it.

'Can I help you?' he asked. Whereupon, the TV inspector identified himself and asked to see his TV licence.

The husband hesitantly said, 'I'm not sure where it is, [bluffing] but we do have one, it's just that the wife isn't in and she would have put it away [still bluffing]. Now let me think – where would the wife keep it?'

To which the TV inspector said, 'I'll save you some time – it's behind the big clock on the mantelpiece!'

The husband went back in and sure enough, there it was. Returning to the front door with his TV licence in hand, he said, 'That's some bloody machine you have that can tell the exact position of where the licence is kept!'

Recognition At Last

• • •

Walking around a car boot sale, I was delighted to find an old *Morris's Motorcycle News Magazine* I had written it about twenty five years ago, while in the police force, to raise funds for a children's charity.

Eagerly picking it up, I thought to myself, 'Recognition at last, I'm for sale in a car boot.' I asked the price.

'You can have it for fifty pence,' said the stallholder.

My expression dropped as I thought about all the hard work I had put into writing it, only to learn that it was being sold for such a paltry sum of money all these years later. Sensing my hesitation, the stallholder said, 'Oh, all right, you can have it for twenty-five pence then!' I looked at him with utter contempt and said, 'No, thanks, mate. I've read it.' Then under my breath I uttered, 'Ya Bastard!'

Alfie and the Star Wars Game

. . .

During one of his many drinking binges, Alfie was accompanied by one of his booze buddies, wee John Scott, or Scotty as he was better known.

As they sat in a small booth in the pub, they noticed that the table they were using was in fact an amusement arcade sci-fi *Star Wars* game, which was plugged into the wall socket and required a pound coin to activate it, in order to play the game.

Alfie and Wee Scotty had enjoyed several *Star Wars* battles that day during their boozing session and when they were getting up to leave the pub Wee Scotty said, 'I'd love wan o' they game machines fur the hoose!'

'Whit fur?' enquired Alfie.

'Cause the telly is pure pish at night!' replied Wee Scotty.

'But, where wid ye get wan frae?' asked Alfie.

'Nae idea, but . . . ' As Wee Scotty was replying to Alfie, a penny dropped with both of them and they looked down at the game machine they had been playing with all afternoon.

'Whit dae ye think Alfie?'

'Alfie looked over at Wee Scotty and said, 'Quick! Grab an end o' it!'

They both grabbed hold of the machine and, as they lifted it away, they pulled the wall plug from the socket.

Bold as brass, they walked straight out the door of the pub carrying the table, completely unnoticed by staff or, patrons in the crowded pub.

Unfortunately for our two opportunists, they only managed to walk a few hundred yards carrying their *Star Wars* game machine when a passing police patrol car spotted them and stopped them in their tracks.

'Look out Scotty boy. The Klingons are about to circle Uranus!' said Alfie.

Wee Scotty looked at the police officers approaching, then looked back at Alfie and said, 'What do you want to do, Alfie? Run?!'

Quick as a flash Alfie replied, 'Don't be stupid – the polis can travel at warp speed.'

'Well what do you suggest then?' asked Scotty.

Alfie paused for a moment, then blurted out, 'Beam me up Scotty!'

Both of them then fell about laughing as the two big policemen approached.

Try as they might to conjure up a believable excuse, the police officers were having none of it and the pair were promptly arrested and, along with their booty, returned to the pub.

Fortunately for the both of them, the landlord knew them as regular customers and in their state of intoxication he saw the funny side of their prank and did not press charges against either of them.

Alfie and Wee Scotty were over the moon by this gesture. However, it taught the landlord a lesson and from that night, all three gaming machines in the pub were chained to the floor to prevent any repetition of their act.

As a final piece to the story, you'll be star-struck to know, the landlord just happened to be called James 'Jimmy' Kirk! (Retired captain of the *Enterprise* perhaps?)

Frankie, The Make Up Artist

A few years ago, I was approached by a traditional Scottish/Irish Folk band and asked to manage them. This entailed organising proper rehearsals, raising their profile and performing all administration duties.

Several months into the job, I negotiated, arranged and prepared to go on a 21 day tour to Moscow, Russia.

This was an exciting prospect, having never visited the country before, but I was pleasantly surprised by the fantastic reception we received and the agent organising our concert performances was very competent and confident we would be a success.

The members of the band were all very excited and up for it, as we looked forward to our first stage performance.

Frankie was the percussionist in the band and very much in love with himself and his appearance. With this in mind, he purchased a long piece of braided hair and would attach it under his own thinning, short hair, to hang down and make him look a cool dude.

Not finished there, he would wear a feileadh-mhor, which is the long tartan kilt material you wrap artistically around you, with leather straps, wrapped around both wrists and legs.

Finally, to complete the image, Frankie decided to give himself the St Tropez look with a cheap bottle of false tan he had acquired from the Glasgow Barras market, advertised by the salesman as, 'The genuine article, cost £49.99 in the shops, selling today for only £3.00 a bottle, or two for a fiver!'

This, to Frankie, who was a total attention-seeker, would definitely make him stand out from the other members of the band on stage, so he purchased the bargain two bottles.

The opening concert appearance duly arrived and the auditorium was buzzing with expectation from the assembled audience who had seen the band being interviewed on Moscow television.

'Where's Frank?' I enquired from the other band members in the dressing room.

'He's just in the toilet boss!' replied Hamish. 'Probably a bit of first-night nerves, but he'll be OK!'

As I gathered the others together and wished them all the best for a good concert, I could hear our Russian promoter going through his build-up announcement of the band, then, we were on. As the others began to file past me onto the stage to a rapturous applause from our Russian audience, I shouted on Frankie.

Click! The toilet door opened and out came Frankie, looking like Michael Jackson in reverse. He had gone in white and come out brown!

With no time to say anything, I ushered him onto the stage and stood back to watch the reaction of the others as he made his appearance alongside them, but like true professionals they didn't make a big deal of it.

However, his obvious change in appearance didn't go unnoticed and prompted the Russian promoter to enquire of me, 'Harry, what is wrong with Frankie? His colour?'

I did my best to play it down. 'Oh, it's just an old army ritual, Vitaly. He used to be in the Black Watch and out of respect he still likes to put on some camouflage now and again!'

Vitaly looked at me totally unconvinced and said, 'The Black Watch?' Come off it, Harry – I am Russian, not stupid. He looks more like one of the Four Tops than a Celtic folk singer!'

'Aye, all right, Vitaly!' I admitted. 'He's overdosed on his cheap St Tropez false tan fluid!' That said, we both had a laugh and then went out front to take our seats and enjoy the performance.

Everything was going fine and the sold out Russian audience were extremely appreciative of the music and songs being performed for them. Then disaster struck for Frankie, who was posing like a complete and utter fanny, trying to look ultra-cool.

Well it would have been OK if he *had* stayed cool, but due to the sweat worked up with the performance coupled by the intense heat from the stage lights, poor Frankie began to perspire profusely and it wasn't too long before his St Tropez false tan was running off his face and leaving obvious white stripes.

There was also another very noticeable mistake made by Frankie. You see, Frankie had decided to give his legs the same treatment, but had rubbed the cream onto the front of his legs, forgetting that you really should rub it on the back of your legs as well. As a result, when he turned his back to the audience, his legs and neck were pure white, which was blatantly obvious to everyone in the audience, bar one blind man. And as if that wasn't enough to contend with, Frankie had also put mascara on his eyes, eye brows and even used it to draw on his very fashionable pointed shaped sideburns, à la Midge Ure!'

'Mascara' should have been spelt 'massacre' – it was a disaster! Poor Frankie – all his effort to try and look the coolest dude on stage had backfired with disastrous effect, and by the end of the performance, what with continually wiping the sweat from his face, he resembled a cross between Alice Cooper and Ozzy Osbourne, with his black mascara, smudged and running everywhere.

The ideal look if you want to haunt a house, but not recommended for a Celtic folk band performing Scottish and Irish music on stage in Moscow, in front of hundreds of young Russians.

However, all was not lost as the band, the audience, the promoter and myself had a right good laugh at his expense.

For his bit, Frankie mixed with the younger members of the adoring Russian audience, totally unaware of his streaky-bacon look until Hamish couldn't resist it any longer and took great pleasure in eventually holding up a mirror and pointing it out to him.

For the first time in his life, Frankie had made a hasty retreat and run away from female company, with no threat of an irate husband or jealous boyfriend in sight. For a change!

Needless to say, he was never allowed to forget it and was regularly reminded of it during performances, when I would relate the story to our future audiences, prompting bouts of laughter and hilarity.

Passive Smokers

...

Deciding to try and do something about my being overweight and my lack of fitness, since retiring from the police, I enrolled with the fitness club at the local sports centre.

Having been unable to exercise properly for several years, due to a serious back injury I had no sports equipment left and as a result went shopping for a 'look at me' tracksuit and training shoes.

I entered a large sports superstore and made my way to the shoe department, on my first leg to at least looking the part.

A male customer was in conversation with the shop assistant, 'I'm no' kidding ye Bob, but by halftime, he was absolutely knackered. He was even struggling to draw a breath.'

'Aye. Ah know! But is he no' a smoker?' asked the assistant.

'He is,' the man replied. 'But it shouldn't affect his breathing as bad as that! I should know, 'cause I smoke as well and I'm all right.'

There was a short pause, before the assistant informed him, 'Did I tell ye that my faither's in the hospital?'

'Is he? Whit's wrang wi' him this time?' asked the customer.

'Lung cancer!

'Ye're joking!' replied the stunned customer.

'Naw! The family canny believe it, 'cause he stoaped the smoking three weeks ago and had stuck more patches on his arm than there is on a home-made quilt!

'He jist bought new a new tracky and trainers tae. He was gonnae join a gym and get fit!'

'That's unbelievable!' responded the sympathetic customer.

'Ah know, tell me about it!' replied the assistant, 'Jist when he managed tae chuck it tae! My Maw's cracking up wi' the Labour Club where my faither drank. She's blaming them. She's seeing a lawyer aboot suing them for passive smoking!'

Answers from Police Scotland Exams

• • •

These are some genuine answers and definitions submitted by police students during the Police Scotland Exams 2004.

1. 'Malicious Mischief is a crime at common law and is when someone steals flowers and tramples on grass.'
2. 'Assault – to strike someone using any part of your body.'
3. 'A House is any place that has plumbing fitted.'
4. 'Indecent Assault – touching yourself in a sexual manner.'

Apparently, just about every Police Officer sitting the Exams on the day, admitted guilty to the definition answer of number (4).

Show Me Yer Jean Brody!

· · ·

A police officer was awaiting his wife coming out of the bath, so that he could go into the bathroom and perform the three S's: a shave, a shower and a sh-sh-shampoo!

After a few moments, his wife entered the lounge with a turban-style towel wrapped around her damp hair and wearing a rather elegant and comfortable-looking dressing gown and sat down, whilst her husband went upstairs, swapping places with her and entering the bathroom.

A few minutes passed, when there was a knock on the front door and the wife answered it.

Standing on the doorstep was David Paisley, a former police colleague of her husband.

'Hi Helen. Is Robert in?' he asked her.

'He is,' she replied. 'But he's just gone upstairs for a shower.'

'Is that right?' he replied, his body language changing. He then said, 'I bet you look absolutely gorgeous under that dressing gown.' Helen was flattered but also very embarrassed at David's personal comments and attention.

'I'll tell you what Helen – I'll give you a hundred pounds, if you let me see yer tits!' he asked her out of the blue.

'What?! What the hell do you think I am, David Paisley?!' she replied in disgust.

'Woah, woah! Calm down, Helen darling. It's not a big deal! You're a gorgeous looking woman. I'm only asking for a wee look at yer diddies! Even just the one – just slip yer dressing gown to one side, so I can have a wee butcher's hook at them and I'll give ye a hundred quid!' he pleaded.

Helen pondered for a moment while thinking over his offer.

('£100 pounds just to see one of my breasts . . .')

'OK!' she said, 'But just the one and nae groping me.'

At that she put her head to the side, making sure her husband was still in the bathroom and satisfied that he was, she pulled her dressing gown to one side exposing her bare left breast.

As she covered herself up again, David handed her over the agreed £100 in cash.

Helen quickly took possession of the money and placed it in her dressing gown pocket.

'Helen! Helen,' David said, shaking his head. 'Helen, that was amazing! Better than I could ever have imagined. Please don't be embarrassed – you have a beautiful body for your age! In fact, I'll tell you what – you've excited me and turned me on that much,' he paused! 'I'll give you another hundred pounds, if you give me a swatch downstairs.'

Helen was shocked and blushed at this next request.

'C'mon, Helen, a hundred pounds just to pull yer dressing gown to one side and gie me a wee peek at yer beaver!' he offered her.

Again she thought for a moment, before tilting her head to one side to listen out for her husband. Convinced he was still in the shower and flattered by her door step admirer, she said, 'Aw right, but ye better no' try and touch me, ya clatty bastert, or I'll kick ye in the balls!' At that, she then pulled her dressing gown up and to the side, exposing her downstairs private parts.

As she again covered up, she said, 'Quick! Give me my money.'

David held up his side of the bargain and having paid her the money, said. 'I'll tell ye what, Helen, if I said you had a beautiful body, would you hold it against me'? Cause I've got another hundred pounds here and it's all yours, if ye open up yer dressing gown and let me gie ye a squeeze and a wee cuddle.'

Helen responded immediately, 'Away you an' bile yer heid, ya bloody sick pervert! Coming to my front door and asking me tae dae aw that! Whit dae ye take me for?' She continued, 'And another thing – whit if some bugger was tae see us?'

'Aw! C'mon, Helen, nae bugger can see us here! Just a wee cuddle, that's all. I've always fancied you big time! What harm can it do?' he reasoned with her. 'C'mon Helen!' At that, David began to sing to her, 'If I said you had a beautiful body would you hold it against me?'

Quick as a flash, Helen responded, 'A hundred pounds?'

'My hand tae God, a hundred quid, in yer hand, like before!' replied David sincerely.

Helen again thought for a moment, pondering over David's latest proposition, while listening out for her husband getting out of the shower and with her mind made up, she said, 'Right!' Putting her hand out to relieve David of his third £100 pounds, she placed it into her pocket before loosening off her dressing-gown belt and revealing her shapely, mature naked body.

At that moment, David put his hands around the inside of her dressing gown and gave her a tight squeeze and a cuddle for a brief moment.

Suddenly, she could hear her husband Robert getting out of the shower.

'Right! Enough! Enough! she said. 'Now bugger off.'

Pushing David away, she closed her front door over and stood for a moment, composing herself as she reflected on her easy earnings, before re-entering the lounge, where Robert was about to sit down in his armchair in front of the television.

'Was that the front door I heard?' he asked her.

'The front door? No!' replied Helen. 'Why, are you expecting someone?'

To which Robert replied, 'Aye! That wee sleekit bastard David Paisley! He owes me three hundred quid for my trailer and promised me faithfully, he would call at the house tonight and hand it over!'

No Age Limits

• • •

George Hyslop, an ageing inspector, soon to retire from the police force, announced to colleagues on his shift that his retirement party would also be his stag night, because after twelve years as a widower, he had decided to remarry.

Everyone present offered his and her congratulations.

'Who is the lucky woman then?' they asked him.

'Mary Brown!' he proudly announced out loud.

His shift personnel were stunned. Mary Brown was a young probationer policewoman in her twenties.

This prompted one of the assembled officers to ask, 'What about the age difference George?'

To which George replied with a straight face, whilst sipping away on his gin and tonic. 'If she dies, she dies!'

The Patient's Armless!

. . .

Early one morning, prior to going off duty after a long and arduous twelve-hour shift, Barry Potts (nicknamed 'Bam') and I, along with the rest of our colleagues were gathered in the police garage when a call came over the radio regarding a train crash at Polmadie in Glasgow.

Everyone present jumped back into their patrol cars and headed for the location to give assistance, where on our arrival, there were sirens wailing and klaxons blaring as all the emergency units of police, fire and ambulance descended upon the area as one.

A quick assessment of the devastation caused, revealed the traction engine and several of the carriages had been derailed and overturned, with the train driver trapped under the overturned traction engine.

The fire service personnel worked away, in an effort to free the trapped driver and using their portable hydraulic jacks, they made several attempts to lift the engine off his trapped arm, but to no avail. Eventually, the Royal Infirmary surgical squad, or as some of the services cruelly dubbed them, the Butcher's Department, arrived to take over the situation.

With the driver suffering post-traumatic shock and excessive blood loss, the decision was taken by the senior member of the surgical Butcher's Squad to amputate the trapped arm to free him and have him conveyed by ambulance and police escort to the nearest Accident and Emergency Dept.

For our part, Bam and I were detailed to provide the high-speed police escort through the busy Glasgow streets.

The Royal's surgical squad crawled under the engine and in dangerous and difficult circumstances, they performed the amputation, thereby freeing the trapped driver.

We then carried out the next part of the emergency proceedings, arriving at our destination in practically no time at all.

As we were about to drive off, a young nurse came running out of the entrance, frantically waving her arms at us, in an obvious attempt to attract our attention. We immediately pulled up and stopped, as she ran over to us.

'His arm!' she screamed. 'Where is his arm?'

Bam and I both looked at each other slightly puzzled and replied, 'We assumed it was in the ambulance alongside him!'

'Well, it's not there and the surgeon requires it here immediately in order to try and save it. So will you go back and get it?' she asked.

In layman's terms, the emergency team and their patient were completely 'armless'!

As quick as we had arrived at the hospital, we had returned to the scene of the train crash and in less than no time collected our missing arm.

Having radioed ahead about our dilemma, a rail worker was waiting for us and on seeing us arrive, he began pointing to himself and holding up a white blood sodden towel. As we drove over to him, he came over to our car with the arm.

'Excuse me, sir, but wid ye just like tae check the fingers on this left arm and confirm there are two gold rings and a tattoo of a highland bagpiper on it?' He then opened the towel to expose the train driver's full arm, which was saturated with his blood.

I couldn't believe what I had just heard, so I asked him, 'What did you just say there?'

Whereby he repeated, 'I want you to check out his hand, because I need a signature from you that I gave you an arm with two gold rings and a tattoo on it. It's just tae keep me right wi' my gaffers in case they had to go missing. Know whit a mean?' he explained.

Bam looked at him and said, 'Are you fucken stupid? Who the fuck is going tae steal an amputated arm, with a tattoo of a highland bagpiper and two rings on it, ya bammy bastard?'

'Well ye never know!' He replied in all seriousness. 'I'm just covering my back and keeping mysel' right.'

'Well ye can get tae fuck, cause I'm not signing anything,' said Bam rather indignantly.

'Fine!' said the rail worker. 'Then I'm not giving you his arm?'

At this point, I had to intervene to calm things down. 'Woah there, mate!' I said. 'Put the arm in the back seat of the police car and don't be so stupid!'

'No way, not without a signature in my book!' he replied.

Bam interrupted, 'A signature! How about I give ye a signature wi' my police baton across yer stupid heid, ya thick bastard?'

'Right, that's it, I'm going tae see my gaffer about you swearing and threatening me.' At that, he began to walk away.

Whereby, I quickly got out of the police car and shouted, 'Wait a minute there, mate. Let's get a reality check here. There's a colleague of yours lying in the operating theatre of the hospital down the road, with a team of surgeons standing around him, waiting patiently on us arriving back with an arm, in order to try and sew it back on. Now unless you've got something better to do with it, like maybe a triple-arm-wrestling competition, I suggest ye give it to me and let me get on with my job of 'hand' delivering it!' (pardon the pun)

He thought for a moment, before handing me the arm.

As I took possession of it, he said, 'Just check the rings and tattoo are there.' before adding, 'I just hope this left arm is the right one.'

There was no answer to that last remark, apart from the fact he had just confirmed to both of us, he was definitely a thick bastard!

As I placed the arm on the rear passenger seat, he shouted over, 'I hope it doesn't fall off that seat!'

To which I responded, 'Don't be silly! It's holding onto the door handle.'

'Armed' with our important despatch, we delivered it safely to its destination with tattoo and rings still intact and the surgeons were able to perform a successful operation to reattach it.

Although Bam reckons they sewed his arm on back to front and he now gives you the thumbs up and thumbs down at the same time!

You're a sick man, Potsy!

My Uncle Tommy

• • •

My uncle Tommy was a Royal Mail postman who, after many years of climbing up tenement stairs to deliver the mail, decided he would go for a job as a collecting van driver.

Not in possession of a full driving licence, he set about getting lessons in order to redress this situation and sit his driving test.

After many hours of costly lessons came the big day for his driving test. Off he went with 'good luck' messages from all his family ringing in his ears.

However, en-route to the test centre his nerves got the better of him so, in order to get back on course and settle himself down, Uncle Tommy decided to stop off at his local public house, where he quickly downed two large whiskies.

Feeling slightly more confident and relaxed, Uncle Tommy continued on his way, arriving at the test centre a short time later.

As he sat in the waiting room, he eventually got the call, 'Thomas Docherty!'

'That's me pal!' Tommy replied, to the examiner, who was standing before him with a pen and clipboard in hand.

As the examiner greeted him, a strong waft of stale Scotch whisky tested his senses.

'Excuse me Mr Docherty, but have you been drinking?' asked the examiner.

Uncle Tommy replied, 'Drinking? In the plural, naw! Drink? In the singular, Yes! As you can see for yersel' son, I've only had the wan, purely for medicinal purposes, you understand, just to calm my nerves. You know what Ah mean, pal? It can be bloody nerve-racking out on they busy roads! Mind you, I don't need to tell you that. You've probably had a few haufs yersel' afore ye started yer work!'

'Indeed I did not! And you can't have a drink either and expect to come along here today and sit a driving test!' said the irate examiner.

'And why not?' asked Uncle Tommy in all sincerity. 'The boys in my mail depot told me you are allowed up to two drinks at least!'

The examiner gave him a stern look before cancelling his test and walking off in total disgust and disbelief.

Several years later, after he emigrated to Australia, I learned that Uncle Tommy had finally passed his driving test, which I found hard to believe, but then again, 'Foster's' Driving Test Centre in Castlemaine, don't really give a XXXX!

Profumo Affair

. . .

During the government minister John Profumo's sex scandal affair involving the infamous Christine Keeler and Mandy Rice Davies, it was alleged that a senior Scotland Yard, investigating police officer remarked, 'Christine Keeler has more fingerprints up her arse, than we have in our files!'

The Traffic Camera

. . .

A man was driving along in his car when he saw the flash from a traffic camera. He figured that his picture had been taken for exceeding the speed limit, even though he knew that he was not speeding.

Just to be sure, he drove his car around the block and passed the same traffic camera, driving much more slowly than previously, but again the camera flashed. Now he began to think that this was quite funny, so he drove even slower as he passed the area once again, but just as before, the traffic camera again flashed.

He tried it a fourth time with the same result, but this time he had taken a photo of his speedometer reading with his phone camera.

Having photographed his speed, he repeated his actions and drove past the traffic camera a fifth time. By now, he was laughing hysterically, when the camera flashed as he rolled past, this time at a speed that can only be described as a snail's pace.

Armed with his phone camera photographs of his speedometer, coinciding with the traffic camera flash, he waited to see what would happen.

He didn't have to wait long. Within two weeks, he got five tickets in the mail . . . for driving his car without wearing a seat belt!

Bethnall Green Escort Duty

. . .

Along with my partner Big Joe Kelly we were performing surveillance on particular premises when we received a call to return to the office as we were required for a prisoner escort.

'Go home, get changed and return as quickly as possible!' said the Chief Inspector, 'I want you both to catch the 4:00pm train from Glasgow Central to Euston Station, London and collect a prisoner on warrant, being held at Bethnall Green police office. You'll return with him on the following morning train.'

Off we went, returning in no time at all, to be whisked off to the station, via the off licence for a much needed carry out for the long train journey.

'What's in the wee bag?' Big Joe asked me.

'I'll tell you later big man! It's on a need to know basis, it doesn't affect you right now though!' I replied.

Once the train had left the station, I was aware that Big Joe was not in possession of an overnight bag, like mine, with toiletries or a change of shirt. I made no mention of it to him at the time, but I knew from experience what was ahead for him.

After several hours, drinking on the train, we had exhausted our carry out and required to visit the buffet bar for some much-needed reinforcements (because we were both greedy bastards) before our arrival at Euston Station. Prior to the bar closing, Big Joe ordered two extra bottles of Grolsch beer, for his morning after, hair of the dog Scottish remedy for hangovers! He concealed them in the inside breast pocket of his jacket, while I visited the toilet to wash my face and smarten myself up for our meeting with the officers who would be at the station to greet us.

On our arrival, we were met by our transport and whisked off to Bethnall Green police office to check in on our prisoner and submit the necessary warrant documentation required in order to transfer him into our custody and bring him back to Scotland.

After the pleasantries involved, I made arrangements for us to collect our prisoner the following morning and then asked our driver, if he could drive us to a public house for a few beers before we went to our overnight accommodation.

Whilst in the process of taking us somewhere, I heard the driver answering a call and saying, 'I have the Detective Inspector and the Detective Sergeant in the car heading for. . .' and he gave our location.

'Affirmative, Inspector Cohen will rendezvous with him there!'

The driver then informed us that the Shift Inspector and Sergeant, wished to meet with us and take us for something to eat and drink. Good one, I thought promotion and a bevy. That will do for me!

We met up with our new escorts, who drove us to a quiet little Greek kebab shop. As we entered through the front door we were shown to our table at the rear of the shop and out of the view of the public. We sat down and the Inspector introduced us to our host, as very important Detectives from Glasgow.

'We bring our guests here all the time.' He said, before ordering up four large brandys and four Special Greek Shish Kebabs.

Within a short time, more brandy arrived, followed by our meal as we all sat there talking about the usual police stuff. However, I was aware that the Inspector and Sergeant, had their food served up to them in box cartons, while our meals were on plates.

The Inspector then explained, 'Well, we're going to leave you to enjoy your meal. Duty calls and all that. I don't have to tell you what it's like!'

They both got up from their seats, drank down the remainder of their brandy and said, 'We hope you enjoy the rest of your night!' As they left the shop, Big Joe ordered up another two large brandies while I concentrated on eating my scrumptiously delicious kebab.

'Do me a Rodney Laver and eat up a bit faster big man!' I said.

'Why?' Joe asked, sitting back in his chair with his brandy in hand, enjoying the ambience of our back shop surroundings. 'This is brilliant, so why rush it?'

'Because that pair of fly bastards, left without putting their hands in their pockets to pay for this lot and I'm certainly not going to pay the bill for them! So gub it down faster, while I think of something!' I replied anxiously.

Joe paused for a moment, then it sunk in, 'Pair of bastards, they're trying to hump us for a free drink and a free meal?'

'Exactly!' I replied. 'Now just say nothing and leave me, to do the talking!'

I then ordered up a bottle of their Keo Brandy to take away in a carry-out and then I picked up a card for the kebab shop and asked to use the telephone (no mobile telephones in those days). I then contacted our escort driver and asked him to pick us up. Then, closely followed by Big Joe, who was carrying the newly acquired bottle of Keo Brandy, I walked out to the front of the shop and stopped at the serving counter, before presenting my hand and shaking the owner's, 'What a meal Stellios, it was absolutely brilliant, Inspector Cohen knew exactly what he was doing when he brought us in here.

'Anyway, just to let you know, I've just spoken with Inspector Cohen on the phone there and he said, to let you know, he doesn't want us paying anything towards the meal and that he will return before you close up to square you up for the entire bill, so let me say thanks again for a really good night!'

'He is going to pay bill?' Stellios asked, slightly bemused. 'But he say you will pay!'

'Well, change of plan!' I said, continuing with my bluff. 'He's changed his mind Stellios and has insisted on paying for it, he's got loadsa money and it was his treat, so he wants to pay it all, so you've to prepare his bill!' I said before continuing. 'That's why he told us to order up a bottle of Keo Brandy. He's joining us afterwards for a drink!' I said convincingly.

Turning to Big Joe, I said out of the side of my mouth, 'Quick, there's our lift outside, shake his hand and let's GTF.'

We then left the shop, entered our car and were driven off.

'Good food in there, but it's a bit expensive.' Our driver commented.

'It certainly is.' I replied, with a wry smile.

'Where to now sir?' He asked.

'Could you take us to a good English-style pub where we can get a decent pint of best bitter?' I responded.

'There's not too many still open at this time of night, but I'll see what I can do for you.' He then drove us to an area where he got out of the car and told us to wait, while he checked it out for us. He then walked up a narrow lane, returning moments later.

'Right, it's closed, but I've told him who you are and he's willing to let you in for a few beers!' Our driver explained. 'Now, walk up the lane until you see a red door on your left and give it a good bang. The owners name is Ranjid, he'll let you in the back door and when you're ready to be picked up again, get him to call me on this number.' He then handed me his calling card.

We carried out the driver's instructions to a tee and were invited in by this young Asian guy named Hamed. We walked through to the pub/lounge area and . . . 'Shockeroony!' It was packed full of our Asian brothers. There must have been about twenty-five or thirty of them inside and guess who they were all staring at? You've guessed it! The unknown pale face dudes who have just gate-crashed their local hostelry. Fortunately, they couldn't understand us and most of them assumed we were probably the latest consignment of refugees to arrive in London. Especially with me still carrying my wee bag!

'Bye the way, what is in the wee bag?' Joe asked again.

'I'll tell ye later!' I replied. 'Now order up the Don Revie!'

With subtlety and the aid of sign language, Big Joe ordered up our drinks, 'Ho, Rancid! Give us a couple o' pints of yer 'breast butter', if you would!'

I quickly intervened, 'Sorry Ranjid! He means two pints of your best bitter, please!'

With all eyes on us, Big Joe said, 'Let's show these boys how it's done!' He then uttered, 'Cheers for the beers and here's tae the queers. Bottoms up!'

He then gulped down half of his pint, only stopping to breathe, fart and burp out loud, all at the same time I might add. Talented boy or what? Then all hell broke loose!

'Fucken hell Rancid! I think a cat's pished doon yer beer pipes!' Big Joe blurted out, while dribbling from his mouth.

'It's Ranjid!' I said, correcting him regarding our hosts name.

'You're telling me it's ranjid!' He replied. 'I've just fucken swallowed hauf o' it.'

He then held his pint toward me and said, 'Fucken taste that pish yersel'. It's bowfin and you know me Harry, I'll drink my beer through a wean's shitty nappie!'

'What do you want me to do about it?' I asked him.

'Fucken tell him. You're the DI efter all, I'm only the DS.'

Undeterred! He then takes another gulp from his pint glass, just to confirm it was 'rancid'. 'Madras! I can fucken taste curry as well as pish!' He said out loud, spilling some of the liquid contents over his shirt and trousers. 'Look at that! It's even taking the colour oot my basterting new shirt! Ho! Hamheid, check this out.'

'Right Joe, cool the beans, it's Hamed, so enough! Drink up and let's GTF.' I said, sensing an uncomfortable atmosphere amongst our new friends, with Joe slagging off their best amber liquid.

'Drink up?' Joe replied in disgust. 'Are ye fucken mad? I'd rather drink my ain urine. Anyways, I'm putting my name up on the board, I want tae play a game o' pool wi' Hamheid and some of his ethnic soul brothers.'

I responded by whispering in his ear, 'If you don't keep yer voice down a bit, we just might end up floating upside-down in a pool, courtesy of Hamed and his soul brothers. Now follow me and let's go. Now!'

I turned to Ranjid and asked him to call the number on the card while Joe paid for our beers, which were extortionately over priced.

'Excuse me Rancid! But did I order drinks for everybody at the bar? Cause I think you've fucken jist charged me for them.' Joe said angrily.

'Forget it!' I told Joe. 'Let's just get out of here.'

'Forget it?' An irate Joe replied. 'Well why don't I drop my trousers and let him park his rickshaw' between the cheeks o' my arse as well?'

'Rickshaws are Chinese ya big diddy!' I said, correcting him.

'Well chapati then!' He responded.

At that, Ranjid enquired in a snide manner, 'So boys, did you enjoy your beers then?'

'Definitely!' I said, 'Very mucky indeed with a distinct taste of keegh to add a bit of body, in fact, it was full of it, obviously a blend of your own special brew. I presume it's popular!'

He stared at me with a vacant look on his face, totally oblivious to what I was talking about.

As I shook his hand, I said, 'Well thanks for that Ranjid and, as we say in Scotland, you've been an absolute tadger of a host and a real douche bag, so you and Hamed have a nice day!'

We then left by the back door and fortunately for us, only our driver was waiting outside to meet us, at the entrance to the lane, so at this point, I decided we would head for our overnight accommodation and enjoy our bottle of brandy, acquired at the expense of Inspector Cohen and his sidekick Sergeant.

Next morning, I arose early and after I had showered and shaved. I went to Big Joe's room and found his door unlocked, so I entered. With the windows closed all night, the room smelt worse than Ranjid's Best Bitter. Big Joe had also visited his toilet during the night and forgotten to flush the contents of the pan.

Sitting on his dressing table were his two bottles of Grolsch beer, for his hangover cure. I quickly removed the tops and poured the contents down the sink. I then filled them up with lukewarm tap water, before replacing them. All the while I was in his room, Joe slept like a baby, interrupting his snoring with the occasional loud bout of flatulence!

His suit was lying on the floor, where he had discarded it the previous night and he was still wearing his shirt in bed.

I then went back to my room to get dressed and put on my clean shirt. With my teeth brushed and my tie straight, I put my soiled shirt and toiletries back in my overnight bag and knocked loudly on Big Joe's room door before opening it.

'Rise and shine big man or you're going to be late for your breakfast!'

'What time is it?' He enquired, in his drowsy hung-over state.

'It's now eight o'clock and we are getting picked up at nine, so you'd better get yer arse into gear and I'll meet you downstairs in the restaurant.'

'Right! Right! I'm coming!' He shouted back.

Having enjoyed my cooked English breakfast I was relaxing with a cup of coffee, reading the morning newspaper, when an apparition appeared before me. It was Big Joe, standing there in his soiled shirt and crushed suit, with his hair tousled and sticking up. He was totally minging and dressed like a burst bin-bag! He then spoke with a deep sincerity, 'I hope we get the same train back up the road!'

'How come?' I asked.

'Cause that wee bastard Dai serving at the buffet bar, sold me two bottles o' fucken warm water, the wee Welsh Twat!'

'You're kidding?' I said, trying to appear surprised.

'Naw, I am no' kidding!' He replied. 'The wee bastard. I'll fucken 'Dai' him. He then looked around the breakfast tables. Anything for drinking here, I'm choking for a hair of the dog. I'd even drink a pint o' Rancid's stale pish!'

'Get yourself a glass of milk!' I said condescendingly.

As he stood there looking at me, looking back at him, he let his eyes focus upon my bag at the side of me, then, the penny dropped.

'I presume that's your over night bag with a clean shirt, toothbrush and a razor?' He enquired dejectedly. I nodded my head and grinned like a Cheshire cat.

'I suppose I look like a bag o' shit, right?' He asked.

'Definitely!' I replied, nodding my head.

'I'm gonnae look more like your prisoner than he is!' He remarked.

I nodded again, still grinning, confirming his statement.

To which he responded rather disconsolately by looking me straight in the face and saying, 'BASTARD!' 'Sorry, DI BASTARD!'

Bloody Witch Doctor!

. . .

Whilst on traffic patrol duty one night with my partner we had occasion to stop a car being driven erratically by a young male in the city centre. We pulled him over and, as suspected, he was under the influence of alcohol, so we arrested him and conveyed him to the central police station where we carried out the procedure pertaining to a drink driver.

During this procedure, the young male driver, who turned out to be a student at one of the local universities, was given the opportunity of providing a blood sample, which would be taken by a doctor, or urine. The young student opted to provide blood and the police casualty surgeon was contacted to attend.

Now, the police casualty surgeon is a qualified GP who has a practice but is also on call to work for the police in any situation where a doctor's expertise is required.

As we sat in the doctor's room in the police station awaiting his arrival, I was completing the necessary forms required and the young student, who by this time had sobered up quite a bit due to the shock of being arrested, was informing me that he had been to a students' union party and genuinely didn't intend to drink and drive. We were still chatting when I was informed of the arrival of the police casualty surgeon.

I remained with the student while my colleague left the room to see the doctor. As it turned out, the doctor was reasonably new to the police system and one of the first black doctors who was to become a regular, on call with the central police station, named Dr Mutu.

Moments later, the door opened and in came Doctor Mutu, whereby on seeing him the young student immediately sat upright in his chair and his relaxed facial expression changed to one of total apprehension.

'Hello, I'm Dr Mutu the police casualty surgeon and I am here to examine you and take a sample of your blood, which I'm informed you have agreed to provide.'

To the complete and utter surprise of everyone present, the student said, 'Not on your life Sammy Davis! You're not taken any blood from me!'

'Calm down now.' Said Dr Mutu, 'I'm a doctor! You won't feel a thing!'

'You're darn tootin I won't, 'cause you're no' touching me, now do a drum roll and beat it – I want a proper doctor, not some refugee as black as two in the morning who's just arrived here in a banana boat!' blasted the rude student.

As he sat back down on his chair with a genuine look of extreme fear on his face, I tried to calm him down. 'C'mon, big man, cool it and don't start acting stupid. You've been fine up until now!' I said reassuringly, but he interrupted me. 'Aye right up until he came in! I mean, how do I know he's a doctor? Let him prove it!' he said, with his voice quivering with genuine fear.

'I *am* a doctor!' answered Dr Mutu.

'Well, prove it, then, let's see some medical certificates, I mean, I've proved to the police I'm a student – I gave them my university student ID card and I also gave them my driving licence to prove I'm a qualified driver. So let me see your ID!' demanded the young student, becoming more nervous.

'But, I *am* a doctor!' reiterated Dr Mutu, annoyed by the fact his qualifications were being called into question. 'Now I'm here to take blood from you!'

'Aye, right, with a bloody big spear! I don't think so, "chief" – away back to your village and shrink a few more skulls for the tourists!' cried the student, who by now had lost the plot and was petrified. He continued, 'Just climbed down out a tree and thinks I'm going to let him stick spears in me, or is it darts you're using tonight, chief? No way, big man, I'm not letting him near me!'

Now, by this time, Dr Mutu was visibly shocked by this reaction from the student, but is still trying to plead his case, 'But I am a real doctor!'

At which point, my partner and I are in pain, trying not to laugh outwardly at the antics of them both, particularly the quiet unassuming student of fifteen minutes ago, who is now acting as if the police station had become Rorke's Drift and we've been surrounded by Zulus.

I was trying to restrain the student and calm him down, but he was still rambling, 'It's alright for you two, saying calm down, but you're not the one being faced with *him*!' he said, almost crying with fear.

Meantime, Dr Mutu is still reiterating, 'But I am a doctor.' He then looked at me for some kind of confirmation, emphasising his words, 'Tell him, officer, *I am a doctor!*'

'Aye, a bloody witch doctor!' replied the student. 'Show me some proof, then. Let me see your medical certificates! C'mon then, show me. Can't do it, can you?'

'I don't carry my medical certificates about with me,' said Dr Mutu. 'You just have to believe me when I tell you that I am a doctor!'

'Sorry, chief, not good enough!' replied the student.

Finally, with all the commotion from the student and Dr Mutu, coupled with the now hysterical laughter of my partner and me, the door opened and in walked the duty officer.

'What the hell is going on in here? You can be heard all along the corridor.' he yelled.

'Idi Amin here is blowing smoke signals out his arse, as well as his ears!' responded the student.

'You just keep quiet.' I said. 'You're in enough bother!' I then stepped outside with the duty officer and explained what had taken place. Fortunately, he had a good sense of humour.

However, the student continued to refuse to give blood and was detained in custody, pending his release later the following morning, for report.

As for Dr Mutu, he went home after a cup of coffee and probably prescribed himself some Valium medication, for the rest of the week, to help get him down off the ceiling.

Later, while sitting discussing the hilarious antics of the student, and particularly Dr Mutu, the duty officer remarked, 'It's only been a matter of time, I've been waiting for it, from some drunk, but I didn't expect it from him – he looked a fairly decent educated young man! Mind you, he'll definitely think twice about drinking and driving again!'

Jackie Barnes

. . .

I'm reminded of a story about auld Jack, an alcoholic who was recovering from a liver transplant and went into his local hardware shop and asked for a bottle of methylated spirits. The shopkeeper looked at Jack suspiciously and said, 'C'mon, Jack, I can't give you a bottle of meths – you're just out of hospital and have a serious drink problem!'

Jack promptly assured the shopkeeper, he was doing some DIY in his house and needed it to clean his paint-brushes!

'But, Jack, I can't trust you – you have a drink problem!' he said.

Jack came storming back at him, 'Look! If my wife came into your shop and asked for a bottle of meths, you'd give it to her, wouldn't you?'

The shopkeeper thought for a moment, then sheepishly conceded to Jack's explanation, 'You're right, Jack. I'm sorry for not believing in you!' As he bent down to pick a bottle from a shelf, Jack said, 'Any chance of getting me one out the cooler?'

The Wedding Party

• • •

A young couple from the East End of Glasgow were getting married.

It was a lovely church wedding, followed by a reception at a city centre bar. Unfortunately for the couple, they both came from very rough backgrounds and there was a bit of an ongoing feud between their families.

Inevitably, after the drink started flowing at the reception, things became heated amongst both parties and a fight broke out. The resident stewards at the bar/diner tried to defuse the situation, but to no avail and as a result, they summoned the assistance of the local police.

The first cops to arrive at the scene, tried in vain to separate the bride's brother and the best man, who were physically locked in combat, but found that the other guests on both sides were verbally encouraging them to continue with their fight. With no solution in sight, the cops called for more assistance, which resulted in the arrival of the support unit.

This is a 'crew bus' full of uniformed officers and cruelly referred to as, 'Rent a Mob', but more often as, 'Rent a Riot'.

The city centre bar was engulfed by a sea of black uniforms, who quickly asserted their authority by force. However, they were unable to separate the two members of the wedding party still engaged in mortal combat.

Joe Logan, the big sergeant, stepped forward to use his physical strength to pull them apart, but had great difficulty as the bride's mother pulled and jostled him from behind and shouted, 'Leave my son alane ya big bastard! He's done fuck all!'

The sergeant tried several times to fend her off, but

some of the other guests became involved and could clearly be heard shouting, 'Maw! Maw! Don't get involved – they'll gie ye the jail . . . Maw! Maw, please maw!'

At that, the mother committed the most despicable of all cardinal sins, by spitting in the sergeant's face. This was a real grogger, or as we say, a 'soft poached egg', consisting of all forms of slime in a glue-like substance.

'That's it!' cried Big Joe the sergeant. 'Jail the maw!'

On hearing this command from the sergeant, two cops rushed forward and grabbed the bride's mother, ushering her outside to the waiting police van. Not the dignified exit she had intended, as she ended upside down at the door with her knickers in the air, screaming blue murder.

The sergeant finally arrested the two men at the centre of the disturbance and conveyed them to the city centre police station to be charged and detained in custody.

However, he was shocked on his arrival when he saw a large number of people, waiting at the charge desk. It appeared that all the guests of the wedding party had been apprehended.

'What are they all doing here?' asked Joe, the sergeant.

'We were ordered to arrest them all!' replied a young cop.

'Who gave the order to arrest them?' enquired Joe.

'*You* did!' replied the young cop, with a puzzled look on his face.

'What do you mean I gave the order?' said Joe, now panicking.

To which the young cop replied, 'You did sarge! You shouted out –"THAT'S IT, JAIL THEM AW!"'

Joe quickly corrected him, 'I gave the order to, "JAIL THE MAW!"'

('MAW' being a Glesca term of endearment for 'Mother')!

Gentlemen Joggers

...

One particular night about half past twelve, I received a call to the Cathkin Braes, an area which was becoming more and more frequented by many gay men. The complaint was, as usual, men acting suspiciously, or as we would refer to it, 'grown men sword-fencing on the Braes!'

As far as I was concerned, if they were up in the Braes, they were well out of the way of the public, however I attended and parked the police car and was having a look around when I saw the figure of an elderly man in his late fifties, dressed in a vest and pants, in the grassed area, among some trees.

I beckoned him over and enquired what he was doing out at this time of night, dressed in his underwear, socks and shoes.

Quick as a flash, he responded, 'I'm a jogger out jogging!'

'It's a bit late to be doing that, sir!' I said. 'And you're not exactly sporty-looking or dressed in sportswear, are you?'

'Well, I am and I run like this all the time and no one has ever complained before.' he responded.

'Well, sir! The complaint I have is not about joggers – it's about grown men acting suspiciously. D'you know what I'm saying, sir? This is an area renowned for men engaging in homosexual activities.'

'Well, I can assure you, officer, I haven't seen anybody like that tonight!' he replied unconvincingly.

I looked at him, trying desperately not to laugh, then asked, 'Tell me, sir, do you always go out jogging in your underwear, Burberry socks and a pair of polished brown brogues?'

'Why? Is it a crime to run in my shoes now?' he replied indignantly.

'Certainly not sir, but your vest and pants are not normal!' I said. 'In fact, you look like you have come straight from Marks and Spencers underwear department, rather than Greaves Sportswear!'

'Well I can assure you I run like this regularly and have never been stopped yet by any of the police in Hamilton!' he replied.

'Hamilton?' I said surprised. 'Are you telling me that you've run all the way from Hamilton to here, dressed like that?'

'And why not?' he responded. 'Are you calling me a liar?'

'Certainly not, sir'! I said. 'But I've put up with enough of your crap, so get back in there and get your clothes on now!'

'Are you deaf?' he asked. 'I've already told you, I'm out for a jog and you're keeping me late. My wife will be worried sick!'

'So you don't have a car parked nearby either?' I asked.

'Definitely not! I've already told you several times, I ran here and I'll run all the way back home as well!' he replied.

Now, normally this guy and his sexual preferences would not bother me, but he was becoming a pain in my arse, so I told him to occupy a seat in the rear of the police car, while I checked out his personal details. While doing this, I noticed he was repeatedly looking at his watch, checking the time, so, being the good public servant I was and, ignoring his protest about wishing to run home, I insisted that I give him a lift a few miles along the road, shortening his journey towards Hamilton. This was to make up for some of the time caused, when I had inadvertently detained him and also to prevent his wife from getting too worried about him arriving home late!

He protested vigorously about holding me back from my other more important police duties, but I insisted. When I finally stopped the car and let him out, I couldn't stop myself from laughing at his fancy sport attire and his futile attempt at jogging.

It also wasn't a particularly warm October night to be out running in your underwear.

However, later that evening while on my patrol, I did observe a very smart burgundy BMW motor car parked unattended in the Braes car park all night long, with, I might add, a neatly folded brown pin-stripe suit placed on the rear seat inside!

Guess who owned that, then?

The Mimic
· · ·

One day while out driving with my four-year-old daughter Samantha in the rear seat, a van driver came racing up on my offside and swerved in front of me, causing me to take evasive action to prevent a collision.

Receiving such a fright and forgetting for a moment about my young passenger in the rear seat, I reacted by shouting out at him, 'Away ya stupid bastard!'

Suddenly, I received a sharp reminder of her presence, when she uttered, loud and clear from the back seat, 'Daddy! Don't call the man a stupid bastard!'

Fighting Fire With Fire

...

In order to get results sometimes, certain cops would take matters into their own hands and deal out their own summary justice. Such was the case in the early hours of Sunday morning, when a silent alarm was activated at a village post office that was being broken into.

With all haste, officers attended at the location, arriving in silence in order not to alert the persons breaking in, and conscious of the fact that one of them was performing as a look-out, on the roof of the post office.

As they approached on foot, under the cover of darkness and totally unnoticed by the lookout, they discovered an extending aluminium ladder at the rear of the building, leaning against the wall.

Quietly, one of the cops, big Jimmy Doyle, climbed the ladder to the roof, where he saw the male lookout at the front of the building, armed with a metal shovel, looking up and down the street for any unwanted persons approaching. He also noticed a large gaping hole on the roof, where they had burst through to gain entry into the post office.

Unseen by the suspect, Jimmy tip-toed up behind him, safely negotiating his way around the new opening on the roof and tapped him on the shoulder, frightening the life out of the suspect. Jimmy then put his hand up to his lips and signalled him to keep quiet, before relieving him of the metal shovel he was armed with.

He then whispered to him, 'How many of your pals are inside the post office?'

The suspect whispered back, in a Liverpudlian accent, 'Just the two.'

'Just the two of them?' Jimmy repeated. Good! Are they armed with any weapons on them?'

'Why don't you ask them yourself!?!' replied the suspect.

At which point, Jimmy whispered. 'So you're not going to tell me?'

'No way, I've told you enough already!' He replied, getting louder as he spoke.

'OK, then.' said Jimmy, pointing towards some high-rise apartments in the distance. 'See that block of houses over there, all lit up?' The suspect turned around to look at what Jimmy was pointing towards.

'Yeah! What about them?' he asked with a certain amount of interest, when all of a sudden, – CLANG! – Followed by loud screams of excruciating PAIN! – Followed by a really sickening THUD!

Jimmy had walloped him on the back of the head with the shovel, knocking him clean off the post office roof onto the concrete ground below, where he landed in a proverbial heap!

As a result of the squeals of pain heard coming from their accomplice, the others within the post office popped their heads out of the hole in the roof to check what was happening and were promptly confronted with Jimmy, standing looking over them, armed with the shovel.

'Don't tell me.' Said Jimmy. Let me guess! You've an urgent Giro you needed to cash and couldn't wait until Monday!'

Summary justice, expertly handed out by big Jimmy!

You're Not Dead!

• • •

My eighty-year-old mother is sometimes lacking in subtlety.

One day whilst walking around the local ASDA shopping store with her, we bumped into my uncle John, whom she hadn't seen or heard from for some time.

'Crikey John. It's that long since I've seen you, I was sure you were dead!'

To which my Uncle John replied, 'Not at all! Doctors Whyte and MacKay are looking after me Flora.'

My mother then repeated it again just in case he didn't hear her first time, 'That's the honest truth – I thought you were dead!'

'Well,' said my uncle John, 'As you can see, I'm not, but then again, he paused for a moment, before continuing, 'I am looking for directions to the spirit section!'

Friends Re-united

• • •

I was asked recently if I had ever gone online and visited the *Friends Reunited* website, to find out the whereabouts of, and maybe recognise and correspond with some of my old schoolfriends from the past.

I responded by saying I had no need to visit the site, as I worked in crime intelligence for years and had first-hand knowledge of where most of them were!

Hughie's Tortoise Room

• • •

While growing up, I shared a room with my younger brother Hughie.

Both of us, I might add, were not exceptionally house-proud when it came to housework, particularly if it coincided with a game of football.

My long suffering mother, (wee Flo) gave up on us and refused to enter our room again to collect any washing until we got our act together and cleaned it up. We had so much lying about you would have struggled to see the floor carpet. I kid you not – Lord Lucan could have been hiding out in our room for years and we wouldn't have known.

Both being footballers, we had dirty football strips, socks, boots and minging jockstraps all lying about the floor. We even offered to pay one of my younger sisters to tidy it up, but she refused to enter the room without the required tropical injections needed for abroad.

Finally, my father big Freddie intervened, 'Both of you get into that room and don't come out until it's clean and tidy and doesn't require to have a health warning sign on the door before your mother goes back in!'

Not about to argue with the big man, we entered our room, armed with washing basket, Hoover, dusters, survival pack, garden strimmer and flamethrower.

Several hours later and umpteen black bin bags packed to the hilt, we discovered we had a carpet fitted to the floor. The room was beginning to look spick and span, apart from the disgusting stale smell which was still circulating.

Two rose bouquet aerosols sprayed into the room with the door closed, made absolutely no difference. It was still bowfin'! We even tried burning some incense sticks, but to no avail.

What could it be causing this rancid pong? Then Hughie said, 'Maybe it's Torty! Maybe his bed needs cleaned!'

'Excuse me, but who is Torty and where did he come from?' I asked, thinking he had taken in a lodger without telling me and denying me my share of the rental proceeds.

'He's the school tortoise.' he replied, 'I volunteered to look after it during the hibernation period.'

'Since when?' I enquired, totally unaware of this arrangement

'Since the summer holidays!' Then he added under his breath. 'Last year!'

'Last year?! And where is it now?' I asked, trying to remain calm.

'Well, it was under my bed the last time Ah looked,' he replied.

At that point we both got down on our knees and looked under his bed, where we found an empty shoebox that used to house Torty the tortoise.

'Where is he?' asked a surprised Hughie.

'He probably couldn't stand the smell of us two and buggered off months ago!' I replied sarcastically.

'Torty! Torty!' called Hughie, as we both started to look for him and it wasn't long before we found him, or should I say, found the remains of his empty shell. Torty was stuck to the floor in the corner, underneath Hughie's bed, like a British Rail pork pie, (A hard shell with no meat)!

He had obviously decomposed over the previous months and hence the disgusting, rancid smell. I was just delighted that it wasn't any of us, although there was a time where it was touch and go!

As for Hughie, He was never again asked to look after a school pet.

Well, if he was, he never cracked a light about it to me!

Chap at the Door
. . .

Lately since I left the police, I have been trying to modify my way of chapping or knocking on a door, for the following reason.

One night, whilst on duty, I received a call to attend at a certain address. I made my way there and on my arrival I knocked on the door, as I would do normally.

There was no immediate response, which prompted me to knock on the door again, this time more loudly, whereby a female voice cried out, 'Yeah, yeah, yeah, I bloody heard you the first time!'

Moments later, the door was opened by a small, frail, grey-haired elderly woman, who, on seeing me standing there, in full uniform, said, 'Do you big bastards get taught to chap doors like that and deliberately frighten the life out of us old people?'

Superglue The Locks

• • •

There used to be an arrogant shopkeeper occupying a licensed grocer shop next door to the police station where I worked.

The previous owner was a very nice man who had a good relationship with the police in the area and refused to sell to anyone appearing to look underage – in fact you had to look twenty-one years of age and over.

He even refused to stock or sell the likes of Buckfast tonic wine and some of the other cheaper designer drinks.

However, the new owner was in complete contrast and was prepared to sell to anybody. He also, very early on in his occupancy of the shop, showed a total disregard for the police nearby and displayed a blatant anti-police attitude. This made him very popular with the local neds and very unpopular with the local parents. It also did nothing to enhance his relationship with us.

Within a very short time the complaints arrived at the office in writing and by anonymous telephone calls, that many of the local underage neds were purchasing their 'Buckie' and cheap White Lightning cider drinks from Warners off-licence shop.

A call was made at Mr Warner's shop and he was made aware of the complaints we had received.

Mr Warner, who was a tall, arrogant and sarcastic character, denied he was selling the alcohol to any person underage and if other people were buying alcohol on their behalf and supplying them with it, it was absolutely nothing to do with him. He also added that if he didn't sell it to them, they would go elsewhere, so he might as well get the business!

It was extremely annoying for the police to learn that a shopkeeper, such as Mister Warner, was prepared to knowingly sell alcohol to an adult, fully aware that he was purchasing it for a minor. Where were his morals and responsibilities as a shopkeeper and parent? Never mind his respect for the law.

Due to the ongoing complaints of vandalism and disturbances being caused by youths in the area, by the indulging of alcohol, we finally set up a watch on the shop to catch Mr Warner selling the alcohol.

Several hours had passed, when a group of about five youths, aged between thirteen and sixteen appeared and gathered outside the shop. Moments later, the tallest of them appeared to gather money from the others and entered the shop. After a short time, he came out the shop, minus any alcohol. The youths remained loitering about outside the licensed grocers, approaching several adults as they entered the shop and asking them to buy them the alcohol they required. The majority refused, but it only takes one and he came along shortly afterwards and, taking their money, he entered the shop, returning a very short time later, with two bottles of cheap wine which he handed over to the youths. All of this took place immediately outside the front door of Mister Warner's shop and in full view.

The male was stopped and charged with selling and supplying alcohol to persons underage. The youths had their names taken, were relieved of their alcohol and their respective parents were informed. As for Mr Warner, his attitude was that if someone was buying alcohol and giving it to someone outside his premises, then that was nothing to do with him.

Charges against Mr Warner were dropped and a smug Warner continued to trade and continued to find ways of supplying his cheap wine to the underage youths of the area.

However, as a final part of the story, the festive period was approaching and like every other shopkeeper, Mr Warner was stocking up with alcohol for his busiest day of the year – Hogmanay. Yes, the day before the start of a new year when we all party and celebrate the end of an old year and the beginning of the next one, with lots of booze! You could hardly move in Warner's shop for boxes on top of boxes of the stuff and he had also spent considerable time and effort making up posters, advertising his special alcohol bargains and tying them to lamp standards, safety railings and even posting them on walls around the area. No matter where you looked there was an advertising poster relating to 'Warner Off Sales'. They had sprung up everywhere overnight.

This prompted numerous complaints from the other shopkeepers within the area.

I decided the following day to make a visit to Mr Warner and confront him with this.

Along with a colleague, I called at his shop and spoke with him regarding the fly bill posting, particularly of those immediately outside some of his competitor's shops. But Warner was a smug and arrogant big bastard, with a total disregard for anyone else and refused to listen, citing the festive period as his busiest time of the year and that he was out to make a killing.

This total lack of compassion and respect for his fellow shopkeepers and his obvious arrogance towards me was disrespectful and I realised during our meeting there was no reasoning with Mr Warner and his selfish attitude.

Therefore, there was no hiding the utter joy and pleasant surprise from the other shopkeepers and a wry smile of satisfaction from myself, when I learned on the morning of Hogmanay 31st December, that Mr Warner had arrived early (8.00am) with extra staff to open his premises for business, only to discover that someone had tampered with the locks of his security shutters and he was unable to open his shop. Now guess to whom Mr Warner turned seeking assistance?

Yours truly!

Try as I might, I had difficulty getting a locksmith who was working that day who was free to attend and when I eventually did manage to get one, the earliest he could come to try and repair it would be tea-time and for that he wanted paid double-time, with money paid up front! Reluctantly, a disgruntled Mr Warner agreed to this request.

Finally, in order to keep him and his extra staff occupied, while they waited for the arrival of the locksmith, I informed him that if he did not attend the main street and remove all those illegal bill posters from the railings, lamp posts and walls, I would charge him with litter and malicious mischief, rubbing more salt into his already deep wounds.

Frustrated and exasperated, Warner had his staff go around and remove all the bill posters.

I would hazard a guess that when Warner eventually gained entry to his premises at about 4.30pm that day, he had a hard shift trying to make up for lost time and revenue, having given all his competitors a clear eight hour's head start.

Afterwards, I spoke with the locksmith and it would appear someone had squirted what he reckoned was superglue into the locks, thereby causing the problem for Mr Warner.

Who was responsible?

Well, Mr Warner made many enemies in a very short time – customers, parents, shopkeepers, etc – but I have my own suspicions . . . 'Evenin' all!'

No Smoking

• • •

An old police sergeant walked into a hotel gift shop and bought a packet of cigarettes. After purchasing them, he opened the packet and taking one out, he lit it up (this was prior to the no-smoking law).

As he puffed away while perusing the gifts on offer, the young female assistant said, 'Excuse me sir, but we don't allow smoking within the gift shop!'

The sergeant replied rather indignantly, 'Well if you are going to sell me cigarettes in here, I think it is only right that I be allowed to smoke them in here!'

The young assistant replied very politely and calmly, 'That's true sir, we do sell cigarettes to customers. But we also sell condoms in here as well. However, that doesn't mean if you buy them in here, you're allowed to have sex in the hotel foyer!'

Happy Clappy with a
Whisky Chaser

· · ·

This story is not for the faint-hearted amongst us!

Prior to taking up back shift duty one Sunday afternoon, my next door neighbour, who was a deep-sea diver, arrived at my house, with a bucket full of fresh clappydoos, which for the uninitiated are very large sea molluscs with a dark elongated shell, similar to that of a mussel. Only much, much bigger!

I decided to cook them and take them with me to work and share them with my colleagues on the shift. After cooking them, I just had to try one or two for myself. They were absolutely delicious.

I then removed them from their shells and placed them into a large plastic Tupperware tub with the water they were cooked in and added some malt vinegar. Once inside the police station, a few of my fellow officers tried them, but a few others were very sceptical and couldn't look at them, never mind eat one. I myself couldn't resist eating a few more. As the day progressed, officers would call into my office to sample my cooked clappydoos, while others, who had never seen one before, would call in just to look at the size of them.

Nearing the end of my shift, big Archie came in and said he had a couple of bottles of whisky and would I like to join him and Beano for a few drams when we finished.

'Sure thing!' I said. 'And I'll bring the rest of my clappydoos with me.'

'Aye, do that.' After finishing our shift, we all three met up to have our drink and a feast of clappydoos.

What a concoction – seafood, in the shape of a large clappydoo soaked in vinegar, all washed down with a large whisky chaser. Totally disgusting I know, but it seemed like a good idea at the time.

Big Archie was the first to get scunnered with the clappies, in fact, within a very short time he was boakin' at the thought of eating anymore and he had only tried one!

Beano, in the meantime lasted a bit longer, however, by the time we opened the second bottle of whisky, he had given up on the clappies, leaving me to polish off the rest of them.

Now, by this time, I wasn't even chewing them anymore – I was stuffing the big clappydoo into my gub and like a Saltcoats seagull, I was swallowing it down whole, quickly followed by a large whisky chaser to help wash it down. This continued for a short time, until I had devoured the last of my clappies and along with big Archie and Beano, we had drunk three bottles of whisky between us.

With the bevy now finished, we parted company. I finally arrived home and went into my house, trying to keep as quiet as possible, so as not to disturb the family. As I leaned over to switch off a lamp which had been left on for me, I stumbled forward and struck one of my collection of decorative wall plates with my head, breaking it, which caused a chain reaction, as the pieces struck other plates below them, knocking them off the wall and smashing them on the tiled floor below.

To prevent any further destruction, I made my way to my bed and as quickly and quietly as possible, I got undressed and slipped into bed. As I lay there motionless, watching the bedroom ceiling spinning around before my eyes, I received a sudden jolt in my stomach. I looked down just in time to see it happen again. This was certainly not normal. I felt like something alien was about to burst out of me, like what happened to John Hurt in *Alien*.

Whatever it was, it wanted out, *right now*!

So as not to disturb anybody, I decided it was best if I got up from my bed and went outside for some fresh air. I went to the back garden and got my Alsatian dog from his kennel and went out the rear gate onto the nearby golf course for a walk! Well actually a stagger!

As I made my way up the course, three steps forward and two steps back, the *Alien* stomach action started up again, then – bbllurrppp! bang! This perfectly shaped clappydoo, without as much as a tooth mark on it came spurting out my mouth like a Scud missile, landing about five metres away, on the perfectly cut lawn of the golf course.

Several other missile births quickly followed this one in jig time, as I regurgitated the lot.

By the way, I never knew I could do this. Talented or what?

In my drunken state looking down at them, they looked like miniature ETs, all perfectly shaped and forming a neat little trail along the golf course toward the green. I half expected one to point at me and say, 'Phone home!'

I remember my dog looking at them, trying to work out what they were and getting such a fright he jumped back that far, he landed in a sand bunker. I had to use a sand wedge to get him back out.

He then looked over at me, as if to say, 'What the hell have you been eating big man?'

After walking for a short time around the course to clear my head and convince myself I was not going to give birth to anymore clappies, I decided to make my way back to the house. As for my dog, he was playing it safe and keeping his distance, just in case.

When I got back into bed, I slept like a newborn baby, farting in my underwear and snoring like a pig, thanks to the concoction of booze and seafood I had consumed earlier. Apparently, I could have peeled the paint off the walls with my breath.

However, when I awoke later on that morning I had a light-hearted chuckle to myself over a cup of coffee, when I thought about the golf course green-keeper, or a golfer on his morning round, discovering this trail of neatly formed sea mollusc aliens lining the course and wondering to themselves, how the hell did they manage to get there?

Now that is what I call a conundrum!

The Medical

• • •

Feeling unwell for several days, I made an appointment to see my doctor and have a check up. After a thorough examination, he wrote me out a prescription and said, 'Right Harry, I want you to take four tablets daily, one in the morning with a large glass of water, one at lunchtime with a large glass of water, one at teatime with another glass of water and last thing at night, washing it down with a large glass of water!'

I then asked him what exactly was wrong with me?

He looked me straight in the eye and said, 'Simple Harry – you're not drinking enough water!'

The Special Olympics

Out one night on patrol in the Castlemilk area of Glasgow, I was assigned a young special constable called Steven – 'Call me Stevie' – to accompany me, while my regular colleague cleared up some urgent paperwork at the office. Now a special constable was a male or female civilian who had a full-time day job and wanted to experience what it was like to work as a police officer and gave up their precious time to patrol a particular area with a regular policeman. This was of great assistance to a stretched and undermanned police force, such as we had in Glasgow.

They would be issued with a full uniform and while working alongside a regular police officer, they held the office of constable and were entitled to perform the duties and enforce the powers associated with that title, all for a considerably small amount of pay – usually a paltry sum and expenses only!

Not every cop liked working with one and felt they prevented them, from getting overtime, due to their presence and as such they would say, 'You wouldn't like it if I came to your work and did the same job as you for the equivalent of two bob, a hat and a balloon!'

I'm rambling on, but that describes a special, so back to the story.

Right, we were out in the panda patrolling, when we were flagged down by a man, waving frantically in the middle of the road.

'Quick officer!' he said excitedly. 'Some wee bastard has just blagged my motor from the roadway right outside my house!'

I pulled over to the side of the road, whereby the man got into the back seat of the panda and I noted the make and model of his stolen car. Once I had noted all the details I was in the process of relaying them over the radio to my station controller for him to broadcast to other mobile stations, when all of a sudden the male screamed out, 'There it's! That's my motor! The wee bastard's driving my motor!'

As I looked up, I saw the stolen Ford Capri coming towards us on the opposite side of the road, with a young man driving it.

I immediately performed a U-turn and gave chase, trying to concentrate on my driving, whilst my frantic male passenger screamed hysterically in my ear, 'Get him! Get him! Get the wee bastard! If he's damaged my motor he's dead! Look at the paintwork – it's gleaming!'

As I closed up on the stolen car, it began to slow down and the driver's door opened. Next thing, the driver put his legs out the car onto the road and started to run alongside it, eventually pulling his complete body out while holding onto the door, he then let go of the car and ran off in the opposite direction. I pulled up and stopped the car allowing my young special companion Stevie to get out and give chase after the suspect. Keen as mustard, this boy!

In the meantime, the stolen car, now minus a driver, was still careering along the dual carriageway out of control with the driver door wide open. Now, if it had gone to the right, it would've hit the kerb and rolled onto the central reservation, before coming to a stop, but unfortunately for the owner of the stolen car, it veered left and collided with the only other thing in sight – a big yellow corporation bus shelter. Watching this entire episode of events unfolding before our very eyes, in what could only be described as looking like it was happening in slow motion, and physically unable to do anything to prevent it, the frantic owner by now was screaming a variety of obscenities in the rear of the panda, 'Ya bastard, ya rotten wee bastard, I'll rip yer basterting head off when I get ye!'

Then as it collided with the bus shelter he shouted, 'Naw! Naw! Naw! No' my baby!' Then his mood quickly changed and he said. 'Aw ya bastard! My motor! That's it – he's dead, he's fuckin' dead!'

All the time he had his hands on my shoulders from behind me and was digging his nails into me. This prompted me to have to tell him, 'Cool the beans sir, you're hurting me!' (the polite version)!

Meanwhile, special constable Stevie was hard on the heels of our suspect, who had run through the front of a tenement close into the rear back courts, which were in total darkness, with absolutely no street lighting getting through to them.

'Wallop', 'Snap', 'Whoosh', 'Bang', 'Thud'! 'Oh ya bastard!' Was the cry! As poor Stevie had forgotten about the dangers of tenants who leave up their clothes ropes and had ran smack into one which caught him around about his neck and spun him up and around like a peerie. I believe he did two triple somersaults, a backward double twist, followed by a half pike before landing spectacularly on his napper.

On an Olympic scorecard, he would score the equivalent of four nines and a straight ten and be in the silver medal position. Not bad for someone who didn't train to do gymnastics.

Olga Korbut would have no doubt been impressed. However, whilst Stevie was performing these spectacular moves and letting the suspect get away, as he thought, I followed him through the same tenement close, in anticipation of assisting him with the arrest of the suspect.

Being slightly wiser and having been caught out by the clothes rope dangers of a dark backcourt before myself, I stopped at the back close entrance, in order to survey the area and allow my eyes to adjust to the darkness. While surveying all before me and looking for some movement I saw a silhouette of Stevie struggling to get to his feet and called out to him, 'Is that you Stevie? Are you alright?'

'I think so!' he replied back. 'But I lost our suspect – he just disappeared. Don't know where he went!'

He had only just uttered these words when suddenly I was struck on the shoulder by a small roughcast pebble from the wall above me. As I looked up, I saw the figure of our suspect hanging out of the stair landing window above, but he hadn't seen me below.

I tiptoed upstairs and, as I neared the window, I saw him hanging on to the window ledge by his fingertips, like grim death.

So I surprised him by jumping in front of the window and shouting, 'Boo!'

The suspect got such a fright he lost his grip and fell from the window ledge, landing with a thump on the paving slabs below, immediately in front of Stevie.

Unfortunately for the ned, he broke his ankle in the fall and had to be conveyed to hospital afterwards.

The expression on the face of the officer on duty at the police station had to be seen, for after the suspect was charged with the offences, he was asked how he had injured himself and he replied rather pathetically, 'That big polis did it, he shouted "Boo!" at me and gave me such a fright, I lost my grip o' the windae ledge and fell aff!'

However! It's just a pity that 'Boo!' doesn't work more often!

Someone To Talk To

Having broken down outside a house, a woman came out to see if she could help me. I informed her it was OK as I had a mobile telephone and had already called for a recovery vehicle.

The woman then offered me tea or coffee, the use of her toilet and generally remained outside in her garden, leaning on her garden gate, talking to me until the recovery vehicle arrived.

As I was leaving, I thanked her for her help and she replied, 'Don't mention it, son, it's only when some poor bugger like yersel', breaks down that I get a chance tae talk to somebody!'

He Fancies You

· · ·

Big Andy was the son of a former British army major and spoke like an officer himself, with clear diction and politeness. When he appeared at the shift as a probationer, I was detailed to look after him.

One evening, having attended a disturbance at a local pub, Andy saw Rosie the barmaid, a cute, petite blonde girl, with Meg Ryan looks and a bubbly personality to match.

He was immediately smitten by her.

'Go and chat to her and ask her out for a meal or a drink.' I said.

'I can't, Harry, I'm too shy,' he replied. 'Would you ask her for me? Please, Harry! Please.'

'OK!' I responded and succumbed to his request. So, like cupid, I sauntered over to Rosie and said, 'Rosie! My big mate over there is a bit embarrassed to ask you, because he's never been out with a woman before, apart from his mammy for the messages, but he'd really like to know if you would be interested in going out on a date with him?'

Rosie replied instantly, in her broad Glaswegian accent, 'I'd really love tae pal, but right noo, I'm sookin' the face aff a young guy fae the Calton!'

"Sookin' the face aff a guy!" Now that was a priceless response.

Ye just cannae dae better than that for an answer.

I went back to tell Andy her answer . . . Well, my answer.

'Well, what did she say? Will she go out for a meal or a drink?' he asked, eager to know.

'She would be delighted to go out for both, a meal and a drink.' I said.

Andy punched the air with delight, 'When!' He asked.

To which I replied with a straight face 'Tomorrow! I'm taking her out tomorrow!'

His face dropped and he looked like he was about to break down in tears, 'You're taking her out!'

'No! I'm only yanking your chain, she's booked up for the future.'

A Word in Your Ear
· · ·

A police sergeant, Ray McVicar, was having a running dispute with a civilian telephonist, Jesse Stewart.

One day in particular, she was deliberately diverting his calls to other extensions in the office and generally mucking him about.

Finally, he had had enough and confrontation was inevitable. He went to the telephonist's room and said, 'Excuse me Jesse, can I have a word?'

To which Jesse replied, without turning around to face him, 'You can have two and the second one's off. Now close the door.'

The Birthday Cake

One particular nightshift, whilst working alongside Big Joe Kelly, I was telling him it was my son Scott's birthday the following day and I wanted to go to a local twenty-four-hour bakers factory, to get a birthday cake for him.

Later that morning, we called at the bakers and I informed one of the staff what I was looking for. Unfortunately, he said there were none left and the ones they did have were ordered beforehand. However, if I came back later, he would see what he could do for me.

On returning, several hours later, the baker produced a cake for me with the message, *Happy Birthday Margaret*, thereon.

'I can scrape off the name Margaret for you and put the name of your son, with a model car or something similar over the area where her name was!' said the baker.

'That's brilliant!' I responded. 'That will be perfect!'

Big Joe then asked the baker, 'Bye the way, who is Margaret and what about her cake?'

'They usually have two or three spare cakes in the shop, so the staff will just pipe her name in cream onto another one for her, although it won't be as fancy as this one,' he replied.

The baker then went off to take 'Margaret' off the cake and returned moments later with it all boxed up for me. As we made our way out to the CID car, Big Joe said, 'So if you have Margaret's cake, what about Margaret?'

'What *about* Margaret?' I said, totally unconcerned. 'She can just have one of the spare cakes out the shop.'

We finished our shift and both went our separate ways to enjoy our days off.

As for my son Scott, he was delighted with his birthday party and particularly his fancy coloured decorative cake!

After my days off, I resumed my duties with Big Joe. Later the same day, we were both going in for our refreshment break and Joe had been muttering on about how that woman Margaret's birthday party went, without her cake? So, when he went to his car to get his sandwich box, I went into the canteen, where another colleague, Eddie McIvor was sitting having his meal. Quickly, before Big Joe came into the room, I briefed Eddie about what had occurred, regarding the birthday cake and with his help, we planned to wind up Joe, with regards to Margaret's cake. We both settled down and were eating our food, when Big Joe entered the refreshment room and sat down beside us.

I then began the wind-up by asking Eddie, 'So how was your weekend, Eddie? What did you get up to?'

'Oh, the wife and I were at an old friend's surprise birthday party down at the Institute!' he replied convincingly. 'It was packed with all her relatives, old friends and neighbours.'

'I take it that she had a good night then?' I asked him.

'It was absolutely superb.' he replied. 'She had immigrated to Canada twenty years ago and only came back this week to visit some friends and family, so we all got together and organised a surprise party for her, knowing it was her birthday and she might not be back here again. What a brilliant night it was!'

'Sounds like it was a lot of fun!' I said.

All the time, Big Joe sat munching away on his food, totally oblivious. So I gave Eddie a nod to continue.

'Mind you! It would have been even better if that baker in the main street hadn't let us down with her surprise birthday cake.' Remarked Eddie.

Big Joe's ears pricked up at this and he suddenly looked over.

'How come, what happened with her birthday cake?' asked Joe.

'Oh! They tried to make out that the cake was never delivered from the factory, so we didn't have one for her. The lying bastards – they probably forgot to bake it!' Eddie replied.

Now I'm sitting there and acting like nothing has happened and not paying too much attention to the conversation. However, Joe was kicking me under the table and pulling facial expressions at me.

He then asked Eddie, 'So what was her name then?'

'Who, the birthday girl? Margaret, Margaret Brown! Why, do you know her?' asked Eddie convincingly.

Joe couldn't contain himself. 'Margaret?' he said, as he started sniggering and laughing nervously, spraying some of the contents of the food in his mouth, all over the table in front of him, while trying to attract my attention with the utmost subtlety. Not!

As for me, I'm playing it very cool, taking absolutely no notice at all and pretending to read a newspaper.

'Did you hear that Harry?' asked Joe. 'Her birthday cake went missing and was never delivered to the shop.' he continued with his nervous laughter.

Without looking up from my paper, I replied, 'And what do you want me to do about it? Call Delia Smith? By the way, I don't think it's that funny Joe! How would you like to turn up at a surprise birthday party being held in your honour and they don't even have a cake for you! Ye're a bit sick, if you think that's remotely funny!'

Eventually, Joe couldn't contain himself any longer, or his nervous sniggering and had to leave the canteen, as the tears in his eyes, with laughing, began to blind him, coupled with choking on his food.

After he left, Eddie and I had a right good old chuckle at his expense and how well the wind up had gone. However, it didn't finish there and when I went to the car to join Joe and resume our duty, he said, 'What do you make of that then? That was Margaret's birthday cake you took for yer boy! How rotten can you get?'

'What are you on about?' I said.

'Eddie's old neighbour, it was her cake you took.' he replied.

I shook my head, 'Don't be stupid Joe – it was only a wind up!'

'Was it fuck! Ye canny kid me. He was serious about that birthday cake. He knew all about it!' replied a convinced Joe.

'Naw!' I said, shaking my head. 'We were winding you up. I set it up with Eddie before you came into the canteen!'

'I doubt it very much, Harry. I'm not that gullible. He knew too much about it and he was even at her party!' he responded seriously.

'Of course he knew about it, but it was because I told him what to say. We set you up, ya big diddy!' I repeated.

'Naw, naw, naw, he wasn't kidding there, he was genuine. Crikey! He even said it himself – he was at the party with his wife! I suppose his wife is lying too?' replied Joe, still totally convinced a party had taken place involving this woman called Margaret.

'There wasn't any birthday party – it was a joke, I made it all up with Eddie to fool you.' I reiterated.

However, try as I might, I couldn't convince Big Joe it was a set-up, or maybe he just doesn't want to admit he was that stupid and was duped so easily!

On another occasion, while we were working together, I asked Joe, 'Do you know where the saying, "What's up Doc?" comes from?'

'Yeah I do!' he replied. 'Bugs Bunny, of course!'

'Wrong!' I said. 'It comes from a film called *Gunfight at the OK Corral*, where Wyatt Earp and his brothers have a shoot out with the Clanton family. Ward Bond played the part of Virgil Earp and Victor Mature played Doc Holliday, who was suffering from tuberculosis and was coughing up blood into his handkerchief. As he did so, Ward Bond looked over toward him and asked, "What's up Doc"!'

He looked at me for a moment, then said, 'Is that right?'

'Of course it is.' I answered totally convincingly. 'I won a pub quiz with that answer.'

Later that evening, as I entered the front office, the station assistant immediately confronted me, 'Here Harry, do you know where the saying, "What's up Doc?", comes from?'

'Aye – me!' I promptly replied. 'I was winding Big Joe up and told him it was Doc Holliday. He believed me and told you, am I right?'

'Ye're right!' he replied, 'He told me he had read it somewhere!'

Not only was Joe gullible, but the big diddy was also a big liar!

The Cigar Man
· · ·

Big Deke was a colleague of mine in the motorcycle section.

I say big, because he was six foot five in height and when he walked, he was very self-conscious about it and tended to stoop. He was a good guy, but gave the impression of being quite a dour and unfriendly character. Coupled with his deep-set eyes, he had an intimidating appearance, suffice to say you would rather he was on your side than against you.

It was a regular occurrence for all the police motor-cyclists to meet up at 3 pm every weekday, in the canteen of the police training school in Oxford Street, prior to carrying out our parking ticket duties, or 'radial routes', as it was better known.

Due to Big Deke's size and appearance, nobody ever played any practical jokes or tricks on him, but he would laugh wholeheartedly at everyone else, when his partner 'Stook', played a practical joke on some of the others. With this in mind, I decided to test Big Deke for his sense of humour, when he was the victim of the joke.

Deke wasn't a cigarette smoker, but was partial to the odd cigar. Now the exploding cigarettes were a regular thing with the rest of the guys, but an exploding cigar had never been done so, prior to going to the training school one day, I made a quick detour and stopped off at Tam Sheppard's joke shop in Queen Street in Glasgow city centre.

I told Tam what I was wanting and he supplied me with this genuine-looking top-of-the-range mega-cigar. This new type was just in and he hadn't even tried them out himself yet, but he guaranteed me it was a cracker, pardon the pun! There was no way Big Deke could resist it!

When I arrived at the canteen, most of the other bikers were already seated around a table, sipping coffee and smoking cigarettes. So I casually pulled a chair over and sat directly opposite Deke. I then nonchalantly produced the cigar from my pocket and was slowly, but deliberately unwrapping it as Deke looked on.

'That looks a beauty, wee man, have you anymore?' asked Deke.

'Nope, sorry.' I replied. 'I only have the one and it's Cuban.' I then paused for a moment before continuing, 'But if somebody wants to give me a cigarette, you can have the cigar!'

Quick as a flash and totally unrehearsed, Deke's partner Stook took a cigarette packet from his jacket pocket and threw it over to me, saying, 'Here you go, Harry, have one of them and give Deke the cigar.'

'All right,' I said, handing the cigar to Deke, who accepted it gratefully.

I then sat back in my chair to watch his reaction to what was about to happen, as he confidently sniffed at it, then wrapped his big horrible lizard-like tongue around it to dampen it down, in order for it to burn slower.

His partner Stook put his lighter to the cigar as Deke sooked on the end of it several times before he satisfied himself it was properly lit. He then relaxed back in his chair, puffing away ecstatically.

'How's that then?' asked Stook.

'Superb! You can't beat a good cigar!' he said, viewing it in his hand. 'Rolled on the bare thighs of a beautiful half-naked Cuban woman – it ranks up there with an orgasm.'

'That good! Maybe I should have smoked it myself then.' I remarked.

Little did he know that this particular cigar was probably rolled on the bare arse of a Guy Fawkes look-a-like and he was about to experience an entirely different thrill!

After several more puffs, Deke was really settling down to enjoying his big 'orgasmic' Cuban cigar and had just put it back up to his mouth, tempting his lips, when – BANG! – the end of the cigar blew up in a small explosion.

I couldn't contain myself, as I burst out laughing, with several others around the table joining me in laughter at the look of surprise on his face, as his deep-set eyes almost popped out their sockets.

'Now you can say you've had a Cuban blow job!' said Davy Holland.

However, fare dues to the big man, who did get a fright, but accepted it in good humour, as a practical joke.

'Were you part of this as well?' he asked Stook, who had, after all, supplied me with the cigarette and Deke with a light.

'No!' he replied, shaking his head unconvincingly. 'Definitely not!'

As the laughing died down and not about to ruin a good cigar, Stook cut off the end that was damaged and handed the cigar back to Deke. He then provided him with another light. Before putting it to his mouth and puffing on it again, Deke enquired, 'Are you sure it's alright this time?'

Before I could respond, Stook spoke up, answering for me,

'Aye! They're just the same as the cigarette ones we bought – they only bang the once!'

Well that's what *he* thought – and me, I might add.

Deke again sat back in his chair, puffing away as most of us around the table, particularly myself, watched with great interest.

'What are you all looking at?' he said. 'If you missed it the first time around then too bad. I don't get caught out twice!'

That's what he thought!

With perfect timing, he took a lingering puff on his cigar when – BANG!!

This time, he got an even bigger fright, and this time he wasn't laughing. He pushed backwards on his chair, sliding along the tiled floor, and threw the cigar as far away as he could.

As it landed on the floor – BANG!!! – It went off again.

He then turned to Stook and said, 'Ya sleekit big bastard, you're out of order doin' that!'

Stook shook his head and tried to defend himself that he had nothing to do with it, but Deke was convinced Stook had been involved in specially arranging it.

Davy Holland couldn't resist adding to the mix by saying, 'C'mon Stook, come clean. It couldn't have worked without your involvement!'

'He's right! You provided Harry with a cigarette and gave me a light twice – you set me up and I know it! You were too quick to give him a fag!' he said.

No matter how much Stook tried, he couldn't convince Deke that he had no involvement and I certainly wasn't going to help him get out of it.

As I quietly slipped out of the canteen, Stook was still pleading his innocence but to no avail!

Not only did I get Big Deke, but I also managed, through his eagerness to help out, to deflect the blame onto his partner Stook!

Good one Harry boy!

Something's Missing!

· · ·

While on police patrol at a busy shopping centre, I was walking about, speaking with some of the shoppers, when I saw a buxom young female coming toward me with one of her breasts blatantly exposed and protruding from her blouse for all to see.

I reacted immediately and took her to one side and asked her to explain this totally unsociable behaviour.

The young woman, stared at me for a moment, then a look of complete horror came over her face and with her eyebrows were raised, she blurted out in all sincerity, 'Shit! I've left my wean up in the canteen!'

It's A Knockout!

· · ·

One night my regular neighbour on the Shawlands Cross beat was off on long-term sick leave and they organised a senior cop from the Gorbals police office, to attend and partner me. Now the cop detailed, was a good guy called Roy Dunsmore, who had great experience and just happened to be a former boxer.

Roy had a good sense of humour and a likeable way of dealing with members of the public, who had drunk more than they could hold and were becoming a nuisance, to everyone in the near vicinity.

Such was the case on this particular night, when we encountered two spoiled brats, who were set on trying to enter a local night club.

The stewards, or bouncers as they used to be referred to, refused them entry. As this was obviously something they were not accustomed to, they were name calling the stewards and becoming totally argumentative towards them.

On seeing what was developing, Roy and I went over and intervened and Roy put his arm around one of their waists and pulled him gently aside, 'C'mon now boys, I think you've had a good night and drunk your last pub dry. So, how about heading home to your bed and sleeping it off?'

The one that Roy was holding onto began to struggle free and said,

'Who the hell do you think you are talking too? I don't drink, so you can apologise to me right now!'

Slightly bemused by this statement, Roy replied, 'Well you both do a good impersonation of a pair of Muppets for somebody who doesn't drink!'

'Are you deaf?' Said the other brat, butting in. 'He said he doesn't drink!' And leaning over to look at Roy's shoulder insignia number, he said sarcastically, 'Cuntstable!' Then they both began giggling and laughing like a pair of nursery-school children.

Roy's attitude changed right there and then. 'Okay boys, you've had your fun, now I'm telling you both to move along.'

They both looked at Roy intently for a moment, before bursting out laughing again. This was not a very good idea! Not in front of Roy, that's for sure!

'I think you pair of mummy's boys better head for home and not say any more!' Roy warned them.

The first one replied rather indignantly, 'Who are you calling "mummy's boys"? I'll get you the sack, you pleb!' Do you know who my father is?'

Roy promptly responded, 'So that's it, ya wee spoilt bastard. You don't even know who yer faither is, well, I'm no' surprised, I wouldn't own up to it either?' At that, Roy grabbed both their arms and led them away before releasing them, to walk unassisted.

'Final warning to you boys, go home now!' He said in a firm voice.

'Who do you think you are, you pig? My family could buy and sell you!' The first one said, as he lunged forward at Roy, grabbing hold of his arm and pulling at him. Roy shrugged him off, but he was persistent and lunged forward at Roy again.

Big mistake!

As nice as you like and as quick as a flash, Roy pulled him around and hit him with a short, sharp, right-hook upper-cut straight to the chin. The spoilt little brat collapsed like a deck of playing cards.

His legs were like rubber and I had to assist Roy in holding him up. He was slabbering at the mouth, as he tried to talk, but was making absolutely no sense.

The other brat, quickly sobered up, on seeing his friend collapse.

'What happened to him?' He asked unaware of what had occurred.

'I think your pal is a wee secret drinker son!' Roy said. As he sat him down, propping him up against a lamp post on the kerbside pavement. 'I think it's gone straight to his head!'

'What will I do?' He asked pathetically.

To which Roy replied with great satisfaction, 'Well if I was you! I'd get a taxi and take him home to Mummy and Daddy, before the same thing hits you as well!'

Roy then looked at me, winked and said, 'Know what I mean 'arry?'

Fishing For Jaws
...

When I was a student at the police college, Tulliallan, the pride of place was an amazing six-foot tropical fish tank, containing a wide variety of small shoals of many different shapes, sizes and extremely colourful specimens.

This wonderful focal point took centre stage in the main entrance of the police college, 'Crush Hall', for all staff and visitors to admire.

At that time my father was also a keen tropical fish enthusiast and I informed the college sergeant of this. The college sergeant had accepted the responsibility of looking after the maintenance of the tank and was busily feeding the fish.

'Well, if he ever has an abundance of fish, tell him I'll accept any surplus he has for our show piece aquarium!' he said.

With this in mind, the following weekend, whilst visiting my parents, I was telling my father about the college aquarium and the request for any surplus fish for their impressive tank.

As it was, he did have some surplus fish and supplied me with three large tropical species called Oscars!

With the fish packed safely in a double layer of polythene bags and wrapped in towels to keep the heat in, I made my way back to the police college the following Sunday evening.

On my arrival, I immediately went to the police instructors' office, looking for Sergeant Lancaster, in order to present him with the Oscars, to add to his impressive array of tropical fish.

However, I was informed he would not be returning to the college, until the following morning.

Armed with my bag of Oscars, I went to the Crush Hall and, opening the tank hood, I placed the bag in the aquarium water, in order to acclimatise the Oscars to what was to be their new surroundings.

Later the same evening, before I retired to my dormitory for the night, I returned to the aquarium and, opening the bags, I introduced the Oscars to their new abode.

I watched for several minutes as the new arrivals swam around the aquarium, surveying every inch of their new home, as they settled in.

Next morning, I arose and headed down to the dining hall for my breakfast convinced that my contribution had earned me some much-needed brownie points at the police college and they would be a good addition and a pleasant surprise for the entire college staff.

En route, I met Sergeant Lancaster in the corridor as he was arriving and briefly informed him of my new introductions to his show piece tropical fish aquarium.

'Great stuff, Morris!' he said. 'I'll check them out after!'

A short time later, halfway through my cornflakes and smoked kippers, I swear the college building shook, as a voice screamed out, '*Morris!* Where are you?'

Not exactly the cheery voice I half expected to hear. I looked over towards the door in time to see a very irate Sergeant Lancaster enter the dining room with steam blowing out of his ears. (that's an anagram).

Lancaster by name and Lancaster by nature! This guy was flying!

What was wrong? I asked myself.

Apparently, the new arrivals which I had introduced to his prized aquarium, had attacked, massacred and subsequently eaten most of his aquatic fish stock during the night and what they didn't eat, they maimed or killed for later, leaving the tank resembling a scene from the Amity beach resort in the film *Jaws!*

Which reminds me of a quick joke.

Q: How did they know that the girl in *Jaws* had dandruff?

A: Because, she left her Head and Shoulders on the beach!

(OK! OK! It was funny at the time.)

Anyway, there were wee bits of fishy heads, tails, parts of fins and bodies discarded everywhere, floating about the tank.

'What the hell did you put in my beautiful aquarium, it looks like it has been blown up?' he asked, trying to curb his obvious anger, as his pride and joy showpiece and main foyer focal point, was reduced to what could only be described as a battlefield.

These Oscars were the *Rambo* of the aquatic world, and this wasn't their *First Blood*.

As I stood there, trying to summon up an acceptable answer, my nerves got the better of me and I couldn't prevent myself from laughing hysterically, as I watched one of my fishy friends, swimming effortlessly past, with a large angelfish dangling out of the side of it's mouth.

As for Sergeant Lancaster, he didn't see the funny side and stormed off to his office. The alternative action would have been to batter me or give me a right good dressing down, I think!

For the rest of my time at the college, I had to maintain a very low profile when around him.

I also had to endure the endless jokes, 'Hey, Morris, I've got an aquarium at home, do you think you could fillet?'

'Good "Cod" Morris, there's something "fishy" about you!' And my particular favourite, 'Hey, Harry, I heard you went out with a mermaid to a crustacean disco and pulled a "mussel"!'

With regards to the trio of Oscar fish, well, suffice to say, they went on to clean up and lived happily ever after, in the showpiece aquarium, within the Crush Hall at the police college in Tulliallan. Alone!

They also continued to grow very big on their seafood diet.

With my intervention and influence, it became a much safer plaice to be!

However, I'm reliably informed that since I've left, the Tulliallan Police College, there's been a remake of the *Codfather* with 'Marlin' Brando!

'Fins' just ain't what they used to be!

Night Out, Now and Again

. . .

I worked with big David Toner, who when off duty, became a good friend of mine and we would socialise regularly.

One night, David and his wife were over at my house for a meal and a few drinks.

During the evening, my kids had joined us, prior to going to bed, and Samantha, my oldest daughter, asked, 'Uncle David, do you drink every night?'

'Don't be silly darling.' replied David. 'Apart from the fact that I couldn't afford it, your Aunt Margaret wouldn't allow me to!'

'Well, how often do you drink then?' she asked him.

'Let me think!' said David, rubbing his chin.

'On a Monday, I go to the police club to play darts . . . and I'll maybe have two or three pints – just to steady the nerves.

'Then on a Tuesday, I play billiards at the British Legion Club and I'll have a couple of pints of Guinness. It's good in there...

'On Wednesday, I'll go to the football and maybe have one or two pints . . . to celebrate or commiserate, depending on the result of the game . . .

'Thursday, I'll stay in with your Aunt Margaret and relax with a few gin and tonics . . .

'Friday, now that's my snooker club night, so I'll go for a pint or two with the boys afterwards . . .

'Then on Saturday, it's my day at the horse racing, so I'll usually have a bet on a few horses and afterwards, win or lose, I'll have a right good bevvy of gin and tonics, washed down with a few beers . . .

'Then, finally, on Sunday, I usually stay in with a carry-out and watch the highlights of the Rugby on television.

'So, the answer to your question, Samantha, is probably "Yes"! But in saying that, you would have to agree, I do like my Sport!'

All For a Packet of Crisps

· · ·

The other night, I called in at my local pub and taking a seat on the stool at the bar, I ordered up a pint of heavy and a packet of crisps.

I sat there for several moments, eating crisps, drinking and reading my newspaper, when an older man entered the pub along with a large Rottweiller dog and occupied the bar stool next to me, where he commanded his dog to lie down on the floor beside him before ordering up a drink.

I was very impressed by the obedience of his dog in reacting immediately to his command and looked down at it. As I was looking at this monster of a dog, it put it's head between it's hind legs and began to lick it's own testicles.

I jokingly remarked that I would love to be able to do that!

To which the owner replied, 'If you give him one of your crisps, he might let you!'

Fun With the Buses

• • •

Several years ago, whilst still a serving police officer, my younger brother Hughie was a Corporation Passenger Transport Driver. In layman's terms, he drove a big orange and green double deck bus about the housing schemes of Glasgow, picking up and dropping off passengers.

It was the practice of all drivers employed on the buses, to save money throughout the year and hold a special sports-night competition, with free alcohol and buffet for all involved. They would acquire a local social club and make the necessary arrangements for their free night of entertainment with monetary rewards, along with trophies for the winners. Through my younger brother Hughie, I got to know a lot of the drivers and on these special occasions, I would receive an invitation to come along and join in.

It was 7pm on the Friday night when Hughie arrived in a taxi to pick me up. He was wearing a white suit and T-shirt to match, in total contrast to me, who was wearing a black suit and black T-shirt. Making me resemble a photographic negative of him.

'Change your suit Hughie!' I told him.

'No way!' he said, 'I look like Brian Ferry in this suit!'

'I don't know about Brian but you definitely look like a "fairy" that's for sure." I remarked.

Anyway, Hughie was not for changing his new look, so off we went on our 'Sports' night out looking like the new *Randall and Hopkirk Deceased!* On our arrival, the committee members who ran the entire event handed out raffle tickets, five at a time, to the assembled drivers, who were present. Each raffle ticket handed over at the bar, was the equivalent of one drink, therefore, five raffle tickets equalled five pints of heavy or lager or any spirit you cared to order.

As the committee member carried out the distribution of tickets, at intervals of every fifteen minutes, he would say to me, 'Sorry Harry, but Hughie will have to share his drink raffles tickets with you!' Then as he was about to move away, he would turn back and, as subtle as a brick to the head, would press ten raffle tickets into my hand.

This would annoy Hughie, 'How come he gave you more drink tickets than me?'

'What's the difference?' I said, 'We're both going to drink them!'

'Aye, right enough. I'll go and get them in. Is it rum and coke for sir, with a beer chaser, or are you on the whisky tonight?'

'One thinks one will enjoy the company and hospitality of one's favourite double act, Mr Whyte and Mr Mackay thank you very much!'

Off Hughie went to join the queue at the bar armed with our first supply of drink tickets.

Suddenly a voice rang out across the room, it was Tommy, 'Are you entering any of the competitions Harry?'

'I might as well.' I replied. 'Put me down for the dominoes and pool. I've trained all week for this.'

'What about the synchronised swimming event?' He said jokingly.

'Oh, I think I'll give it a miss tonight, Tommy, my bikini top has a rip in it anyway!' I replied.

During the events of that evening I was beaten at the dominoes, that bloody double six beat me every time. Anyway, I was waiting to take part in the pool games.

Whilst sitting there, draining every drop of the amber liquid from my refillable glass, with my brother Hughie seated alongside me, a greasy long-haired male appeared. He was wearing a bright blue- coloured jacket with the sleeves rolled up to the elbow so as to reveal several pieces of what looked like barbed wire wrapped ever so ridiculously around his forearm. To crown it off he had a large brass crucifix dangling from his neck. It was that heavy I would reckon that within six months he would resemble the Hunchback of Notre Dame with a dowager's hump.

He sat down in the chair beside me and said, 'So are you on the buses too?'

'No!' I replied.

'Oh right,' he said, nodding his head. 'What do you work at then?'

'I'm a lorry driver.' I responded.

His eyes opened wider, 'A lorry driver? I've always wanted to be a lorry driver. What kind of lorries do you drive then?' He enquired.

'A Scania 110.' I answered.

'A Scania 110? That's my favourite lorry of all time. How long is it and how many wheels does it have?'

Now, at this point I'm thinking, this guy is just out for the day, where's his psychiatric nurse. He was obviously a lump of wood in an earlier life! Anyway, I turned to Hughie and on seeing my facial expression change, Hughie got up from his seat and walked over to another bus driver friend and said, 'Here Archie, yer mental brother is annoying oor Harry, so ye better have a word with him and tell him to do a drum roll and "beat it".'

As Hughie returned to his seat on the opposite side of me, Archie signalled to his brother to come over and said, 'See that bloke ye're talking tae, he's a polis, so don't annoy him, awright?'

Conversation finished, Archie's brother comes back over and sits down on his seat next to me. He then composed himself, looked both ways and behind himself before staring me right in the face. He then winked and whispered in a low voice out of the side of his mouth.

"I always wanted to be a Polis"!

At which point, I turn my head around to look at Hughie and Hughie said under his breath, 'Lean your head forward as if to pick up your pint and I'll just hook him.'

As it turned out, he was quite a nice lad, although slightly demented. Also, apart from the barbed wire wrapped around his arms, posing as some sort of modern jewellery, he had a set of motor vehicle battery jump leads tied in a neat knot around his neck like a fashion statement.

'Why the jump leads around your neck?' I asked him.

'I forgot that you needed to wear a tie tonight and these were all I could find in the boot of the car!' He replied.

'Awright!' I said. 'Well you better not "start" anything in here!'

Hughie then spotted the buffet being uncovered on the display tables by Big Andy Hunter, nick-named Billy Bunter, he was enormous and rumour had it that he was originally a triplet, but he ate the other two. When he was at school, his favourite instrument was the dinner bell.

Hughie moved swiftly to the front of the queue and shouted over to me, 'Harry! Do you want toad-in-the-hole wi' some salad?'

'If you don't mind Hughie, I'll just have the salad, I've been towed-in-the-arse once and didn't really enjoy it!' I responded.

The assembled queue of drunken bus drivers laughed in unison.

Much later, after the buffet was cleared away and many, many more whiskies were consumed by yours truly, I was summoned to the pool table to play my first game.

'Right Harry,' said the organiser. 'You're on this side with the rest of the OMOs here.'

'Ho!' I said, taking great exception to this remark. Then Hughie explained what he meant by OMO – One Man Operator – bus drivers and not HOMO as in a sexual preference.

Surprisingly, with Hughie's coaching skills, I win it very easily. My next couple of games go the same way, as I find it all so easy. The balls as they say are running kindly for me and are never too far from a pocket to pot them into.

I'm playing like Stephen Hendry, minus his plooks and before I know it, hey, I'm in the semi-final stage of the tournament and I find it very hard to believe, because I can hardly see the pool table, never mind the coloured balls. Anyway, my opponent breaks off and I'm bent down, lining up my cue for my first pot at a ball.

'Hold it Harry!' Hughie said, 'Pot this one first!'

I looked over to see one of my balls covering a pocket and just perfect for potting.

'I never noticed that one, thanks Hughie.' I replied.

The game continued in this vein for several shots, me bending down to line up a pot and Hughie changing my mind by pointing out a much easier pot to take on. 'I must have drunk more than him!' All the time Hughie was talking one load of utter pish to my opponent, who was having to use all his concentration skills just to understand what Hughie was saying to him. As for me, I'm closing one eye and trying to focus on my cue ball as it appears to be moving about the table on it's own and I'm thinking to myself, 'I wish that bloody white cue ball would stop moving!'

Then just as I am about to take my shot, I clearly see a hand lift up one of my balls and place it in front of the pocket. I straightened up and composed myself, because I decided, I must be seeing things, balls don't move about by themselves and even in my rapidly drunken state, I couldn't 'piss this mot.' I mean I couldn't miss this pot!

Then I realise why I'm so good at pool all of a sudden. My brother Hughie was talking to my opponents and while distracting them he was placing my balls over the pockets for me to pot them, as well as 'potting' a few of my balls into his own trouser pockets.

I wondered how some games seemed to be over very quickly . . . I was only potting half my quota of balls, compared to my opponent's full quota.

Being a conscientious police officer with a reputation for being honest and upholding the law, I couldn't handle the fact that I was in the pool final due to the behaviour of my brother, Hughie, who was blatantly cheating. With this preying on my mind, I did the only honourable thing available to me!

No I didn't own up, are ye daft? I was winning. I just compromised.

I told Hughie I didn't want his help in the final because I was good enough to win it on my own. Suffice to say, I didn't win the final and to rub salt into my wound, I played total crap and was completely whitewashed. Come to think of it, even when I play sober, I'm total crap. Which, in retrospect was probably a fair result for me. However, Hughie reckoned I was extremely lucky to get nil! Which was hurtful, because I do have feelings you know!

In the meantime, during the evening, Hughie had also been helping the committee by handing out the drink raffle tickets as well as helping himself to several sheets for doing it. He had also arranged with the girl behind the bar to allow us to trade them in for a carry-out and had placed an order for a bottle of whisky, a bottle of rum and two dozen cans of Red Stripe lager. Just in case we got thirsty on our road home.

I decided we should go for a Chic Murray (an Indian curry) and told Hughie I was going outside for some fresh air, while they were clearing up the tables. Unfortunately, I forgot to mention to him about going for the Chic Murray.

While sitting on a wall outside waiting for Hughie, a police panda car pulled up alongside me.

'Hi Harry,' said the passenger. 'What are you doing here?'

'Oh hi Davie!' I replied. It was a friend I had been to college with. I continued, 'I've got this theory, Davie, that the world revolves on an axis, so if I wait here long enough, my house will pass by and I'll get hooked up by the wife!'

'Don't think so Harry, why don't you jump in the back and we'll give you a lift? He said.

'Okay Davie.' I said, getting into the rear of the car.

'Could you drop me off at the Noor Mahal Indian restaurant in Shawlands, I feel like a wee Chic Murray afore I go home.'

'No problem Harry!' replied Davie and he promptly drove me to the restaurant dropping me off outside the front entrance. As I entered I was shown to a table for two as I had told them that my brother Hughie would be joining me here.

All I remember after that, was the waiter nudging me and saying, 'Excuse me Harry, but we are wishing to go home now and I don't think your brother is coming!'

I looked around me and the restaurant was empty, apart from the staff, still clearing up.

'What time is it Zaffar?' I asked the manager.

'Very late Harry, quarter-to-one in the morning, you have been sleeping for ages!' He replied.

While all this was going on, Hughie had come out of the club looking for me, couldn't find me and organised a small search party of his friends to help him search the nearby golf course, just in case I had fallen into a bunker. Having no success in finding me, he then flagged down a 'fast-black' taxi and went to my house, where he informed my wife as follows, 'I've lost him, I've lost Harry. One minute he was there and the next minute, "Poof" he was gone.'

Mind you, 'Poof' I think was the wrong choice of word to describe my disappearance from outside the club.

He continued explaining, 'I've been up and down the golf course next to the club looking for him in case he fell into a hole!'

'Some of the guys helping to look for him nearly shit themselves and ran off when they saw me dressed in white coming towards them in the darkness!'

All the while, my missus stood with her arms folded, listening to this pathetic tale of woe from my drunken brother and totally unconcerned.

Poor Hughie, he was completely demented and unaware, that I was wrapped up, as snug as a bug in a rug, in the spare room of my parent's house and snoring away like the proverbial pig, with my runners up medal for the pool competition along with a crisp twenty pound note tucked away in my breast pocket.

Roll on the next games night on the buses!

'Fares Please'!

And Finally

A Festive Treat......

Harry's Whisky Mince Pie Recipe!

1 pint of filtered water
2 dessert spoons of sugar (or honey)
4 nobs of butter (or one big lump)
1 big skoosh of lemon juice, hand squeezed
6 large free range eggs. (Caged if you can't find them)
1 packet of cashew nuts
2 cups of dried fruit. (anything lying about the fruit bowl)
2 bottles of Whyte and Mackay whisky (Or more).

Having ticked off everything required for the recipe, we'll start off by sampling the whisky in a large glass just to check the texture and the quality of the mature blend, making sure it's not 'corked'.

Take a large bowl from the cupboard and before you do anything with it, just check the quality of the other bottle of whisky, this is very important (a second opinion always helps to guarantee you have made the right choice, so just try it again).

Pour yourself a good measure and swallow it straight down.

Oh, lovely! What a good choice Harry . . . Thank you Harry. (Talking to myself already).

Right! Switch on the electric mixer. (Remembering to plug it in first.)

Beat up 8 ounces of butter in a large fluffy bowl . . . No problem for me!

Add one teaspoon of cake essence, before setting about it again with your whip . . . Sorry, whisk . . . Sounds like whisky!

That was a wee prompt, so at this point, it is advisable to check that the whisky is still okay, so pour yourself another good measure using the same glass.

Turn off the mixer thingy and break two legs before adding to the ball and chucking away the dried fruit. (Whit a lot o' pi** . . .pith!)

Pick up some of the dried fruit from the floor and . . . do what you want . . . you can eat it as part of your fifteen a day! Apparently, it's good for your bowls.

Mix the turner on, and if anything gets stuck in the beaters, use a drew scriver to pry them loose. Hic!

Oops, sorry about that. Hic! I think I've Hic! Got the Hic! I have Hic!

I better open the second bottle of whisky again to check its tonsisticity, (That's easy for you to say). Now hold your breath for 30 minutes, then sift two spoonfuls of salt . . . Salt? Where did the salt come from?

Actually, I think it means malt! . . . Talking about malt, I better check the whisky again . . . Don't want it going off in the heat!

Shift the lemon juice and sprain your nuts, before adding a table!

Add a drop of sugar, or was it salt? . . . Wimp to a paste or whatever, I'm not very sure, but hey it's 'Christmas wine, thistletoe and slime' . . . Burrpp! . . . Ooops, sorry about that one! Wee bit o' windy pops slipped out there.

Make some toast. That's it . . . Toast! Make a toast, so pour yersel' another hauf . . . Let's make it a double this time, we're all friends after all . . . Cheers!

BUMPPP! Oh ya bugger. Who left that cupboard door open? That was sore, but . . . Hey . . . 'Pick yourself up, dust yourself off and start all over again!' Cheers!

Right! What have we not used yet? Oh, ah can't remember . . .

However . . . at this point, it's a good ikea to pour yourself a wee goldie!

Oh, hold on there, I remember now, you greash the oven and burn the cake tin to 360 degrees, trying not to fall over, 'cause it's very slippy in there and I've already got a big lump on my napper . . . Hic!

Crikey . . . ! Would you look at that . . . There's rabbit shit all over the bloody floor . . . ! Where did the rabid comfy?

Cancel that! False alarm . . . Ah've just tasted it . . . It's only raisins, but a good likeness . . . You could be easily fooled, like me!

Right! Whit noo? . . . Oh aye, very impotent. Add a desperate spoon of whisky to the stuffy mix in the bowel.

Now, if you haven't got a spoon . . . just spit in about a mouthful, but not a full mouthful. Ye don't want to waste guid whiksy. Ah mean to say, it's only a bloody cake after all.

A bit of advice here. Don't eat any of the nuts before you do this, 'cause it's a waste of 'Catch-ewes'! And makes one a helluva mess . . . Looks like some pebble-dash has been spilt all o'er it. But more importantly, you don't want floaters in your whiksy grass.

So, remember, it's almost a mouthful of whiksy and gargle it first.

Don't want tit to be too wet! . . . So swallow some of it for good luck.

Now for goodness sakes, don't forget to thingy, you know, 'cause every bugger I tell always forgets to do that . . . Even me! And it's my recirpee, Hic! . . . That's they bloody hiccups back again . . . Ah need a fright! . . . Where's the mother-in-law when ye need her! Ah call her the exorcist. Cause every time she comes o'er for the weekend, by the time she leaves on the Sunday: There's no' a spirit left in the hoose!

Right, where was I? . . . Oh aye . . . Presentation time . . . The finale!!

Finally, pour the fish bowl through the window and finish off the reminder of the boozc and make sure ye stuff the oven in the dishwasher before ye pass out on the floor!

Yc now what wormen are like if ye leaf a mess in their pre, pre, pre . . . How do ye spell precious? . . . In their kitchen.

PS, I've newer massaged to cake a make yet, but it sounds lick somethink I'd really enploy! In saying that, can a sujgest you buy one from Arsda or SAintberrys . . . much chipper and lesss messi . . . Wee Messi! He's good in't he boys?

CHERRY MISTMAS VERYDOBY! HIC!!

And a Harry 'F' word to Goradon Rasmay . . . Get oot my kitchen . . . Ya big diddy!

Well that's it for this shift . . .

EVENING ALL!

PS, Look out for The Best of Harry the Polis, 'The Last Night on the Beat' Volume Two........Coming soon.

THANK YOU

THE END